GLOBALIZATION AND TERRORISM

Death of a Way of Life

Lionel F. Stapley, PhD

D1477578

KARNAC

First published in 2006 by
Karnac Books
118 Finchley Road, London NW3 5HT

Copyright © 2006 by Lionel Stapley

British Library Cataloguing in Publication Data

A C.I.P. for this book is available from the British Library

ISBN10: 1 85575 481 9
ISBN13: 978 1 85575 481 2

Typeset by RefineCatch Limited, Bungay, Suffolk
Printed in Great Britain

www.karnacbooks.com

CONTENTS

PREFACE

Members of societies throughout the world are currently experiencing massive, unprecedented, changes in their way of life. Changes that are lacking in focus, which are on a grand scale, and are of such a nature as to be affecting most aspects of life. Some of the identifiable changes include: societies turning away from paternalistic to maternalistic leadership; countries divided by political allegiance; young people demonstrating; immigration on a global scale; and loss of confidence in political and social institutions and leaders. But precisely what is happening and why are difficult questions for all of us who are involved in this process to answer. This book seeks to show that, these sometimes-violent disturbances to people's way of life are a consequence of Globalization. The aim of the book is to provide explanations as to why Globalization is affecting the world in this way; and to contribute to an understanding of the seemingly irrational dynamics that are currently affecting societies throughout the world. Not least, those dynamics that result in global terrorism by Muslims.

This will involve showing the way that one society or culture, that of the West ("*us*"), responded to a period of economic failure by seeking to utilize global resources—human and physical—to create wealth and to provide cheap goods which would ensure the continuance of our standard of living. At least, that was the openly stated theory of Globalization at the outset. But as we shall see, it was and is, much more than just an economic model. It is a process that has no less a purpose than an attempt to change the world. It is regarded as a process in which technology, economics, business, communication and even politics will dissolve the barriers of time and space that once separated a people—and that the process of Globalization will ultimately lead to the closer integration of the world.

As an economic model Globalization has, by various measures and according to various commentators, been regarded as a success. Among other successes attributed to Globalization is the claim of a rise in living standards that has occurred as barriers between nations have fallen. However, it is also accepted that despite a resulting escape from poverty by millions of people in those places that have joined the world economy, it is still hard to convince publics and politicians of the merits of Globalization. As with many large-scale change processes at both a national or international level, what seems not to have been considered is the effect that these changes would have, and continue to have, on the various societal cultures throughout the world. It would appear that in developing and implementing Globalization the West has not considered the political and social consequences both in Western and in non-Western societies. Or if they have been considered, and there is some evidence for this view, they were totally misguided and developed solely from a monocular perspective; the singular view of the West. As we shall see there have been many effects of Globalization: the most dramatic and representative of all being that of global Muslim terrorism.

The effects of terrorism are, by their very nature, intended to be sensational. And such is the nature of terrorist activities carried out in recent years that members of societies throughout the world will be well aware of these events and their consequences. The resultant deaths and the physical and psychological maiming of those who have survived are plain for all to see. And, being in the eye of the visual news media the images are there to be seen unedited, with a shocking immediacy, and numbing reality by millions across the world. These atrocities are all reported in both the tabloids and the quality news media with headlines that match the shocking nature of the crimes. And the tabloids in particular will frequently respond by tapping into the emotions of the public by expressing hatred for the perpetrators who are identified as barbarians.

The resulting loss of human lives and appalling injuries suffered by the victims of terrorist acts provides a continuing drama as the families and close friends of the victims try to come to terms with the sudden and violent intrusions into their lives. This, in turn, provides continuing material for the news media, as does information about the search for those responsible for such heinous crimes. With each step of the process of grieving and mourning the vivid images are repeated on television and in the other news media. Taken together, they all contribute to a general sense of fear and anxiety by members of society. Put briefly, the effects of terrorism are simply terrifying and unavoidable.

Unlike terrorism, the effects of Globalization may not be so obvious and so readily identifiable. Such is the nature of change resulting from Globalization that it is, in the main, imperceptible to most at this time. The effects of Globalization have nothing of the immediacy and sensationalism that results in terror being so frequently featured in the visual and written media. On the contrary, reporting of items about Globalization is generally confined to the Business Sections of the quality newspapers. Seldom, if ever, does Globalization feature on the visual media and it is even less likely to be referred to in the tabloid press. I would suggest that if members of Western societies were asked about their views on Globalization most would probably be neutral—expressing neither good nor bad views. Some liberal minded members of societies might take a political view that was against the notion of big business and conglomerates because they perceived them to unfairly disadvantage the world's poorer nations. But I would be very surprised if anyone were to offer the view that Globalization could be causing a degree of anxiety and suffering, in both Western and non-Western societies throughout the world, that was experienced as worse than the effects of acts of terrorism. Yet, this view which may be regarded by many as astonishing is that which is put forward in this book.

I should stress that this is not a political view. On the contrary, this book does not take and does not seek to support any party political view whatsoever. But it does take a different approach to those normally adopted. An approach based on an analysis of societal dynamics over the past four or more years. This analysis is unlike many other contemporary analyses as it most importantly contains the psychological aspects of societies as well as the social. Put another way, this approach is what we might term a psycho-social approach. However, before providing some further information about this approach it may be helpful to briefly refer to the reasons why such an approach is considered necessary.

Perhaps we should not be surprised that a project largely or mainly driven by economics should take a rational approach that sees things in a cause and effect manner. This follows the predominant approach to learning in the Western world, one which is greatly influenced by centuries of philosophical and scientific thinking which demands that subjects of study be broken down into measurable units which can then be subject to tests such as those of verification and replicability: a world of quantitative analysis. An approach that is in turn reinforced by our education system that is based upon a successful but ultimately reductionist philosophy of science. It is further reinforced in organizations where technological advances have had the effect of inadvertently reducing the humanistic aspects of management. A result is that we are greatly influenced by (the irrational) expectations that we hold as citizens and politicians (or employees and managers) that formal strategies and structures as represented by politicians (or managers) can offer the right answer (a cure) for all societal (or organizational) problems.

The dominant way of making sense of the complex organizational and societal situations that we face is by concentrating on the rational and predictable aspects of human experience. Indeed, we might even ask why those involved in a largely numerate discipline should have an awareness of the human sciences. The problem is that the results of their work inevitably have an impact on societies as a whole. We frequently read statements attributed to those supporting Globalization based on this rational approach. A typical example would be on the following lines: the merits of openness are so obviously beneficial in reducing barriers between nations and reducing poverty that it would be insane not to continue to adopt such a process. Seen from a rational economic perspective that sort of statement seems to make sense. However, it is to ignore the irrational that exists in all societies that are largely and mainly concerned with issues of culture. As will be further discussed throughout the book, messing with culture is likely to result in huge resistances that may be experienced as irrational. By way of example, if we look at the findings of research regarding so-called attempts at culture change in organizations, we will be aware that something in the region of 90% or more such efforts fail.

We of course need to accept that the dominant approach may be appropriate in certain circumstances but there are others where such an approach is totally inappropriate. This is particularly so in matters concerning human behaviour where in addition to data that is available to us through our usual processes of perception we also need to consider material arising from our internal world. So, what is it that we are we trying to understand? In simple terms, we are trying to understand processes of human behaviour, which by their very nature are dynamic; that is they exist in a state of flux and are characterized by spontaneity, freedom, experience, conflict and movement. So how do we study these dynamic processes? What is absolutely clear is that the value-free, value-neutral, value-avoiding model of science that was inherited from physics, chemistry and astronomy where it was necessary to keep the data clean, is quite unsuitable for the scientific study of life. When we extend science to the extreme difficulties of biological behaviour, human emotion and social organization, then other sources of insight and methodologies beyond those of the empirical analytical scientific method must be sought.

To achieve our aims means that we need to not only be aware of the rational processes occurring in societies, we also most importantly need to understand the irrational, sometimes unconscious processes that are occurring beneath the surface. Those processes that also have such an important effect on our lives and on our societies. This beneath the surface world is what we might term a parallel world, a different world, not so obvious but every bit as influential. Bhaskar (1975) pointed out that the social scientist can only say as much as the tools at his disposal or those which he chooses to use. The tools used here to provide the sought-after explanations are concepts derived from psychoanalysis and systems theories which I believe provide explanations for human behaviour that are both consistent and comparable. This approach has also been called "systems-psychodynamics". I will gladly acknowledge that working in this way is not a perfect art. However, by adopting this approach we can discover enough of the underlying dynamics of the total situation to enable us to gain an awareness of societal dynamics.

The concept of "psychosocial" draws attention to the fact that what we are dealing with in social system transitions is fundamental change at two distinct levels at the same time and that the principles by which change takes place at each of these levels are quite different. At one level are the "social" factors: the products and services, the technologies, the organizational structures, policies, rules and procedures that are the stuff of people's everyday life and work, the external realities around them. These are the limit of most others' forms of enquiry and they operate according to principles that may be technical, economic, sociological, legal, or environmental in nature. This is an important level but is only partial.

At the other level are the "psycho" factors: the beliefs and values, the hopes, anxieties, and defence mechanisms, the ideas and ways of thinking of these same people that both determine how they perceive the external realities and shape their actions towards them. These are phenomena of subjective experience located within the minds of people, and they operate according to the principles of psychology, especially those studied in the fields of social cognition and psychoanalysis. To gain a deeper understanding of societal dynamics we need to consider both levels together. These two levels, the external and internal worlds of people—are in continual interaction: what goes on in the minds of people is partly reactive to what happens around them, but is also very much proactive. People's ideas and ways of thinking influence the way they act upon their surroundings to bring about change in them (Amado, 2001; Rice, 1990).

Applications of this approach that will be explained in more detail in Chapter One have revealed information that is imperceptible to the vast majority of people. For example, a January 2004 analysis of societal dynamics showed that "The reported experience regarding the nature of social change is such that one can only conclude that it is in the nature of a revolution. The depth and quality of change that causes members of society to refer to feelings of de-Christianization, dehumanization and a loss of known values, an unravelling of the social threads that have held us together, can only be regarded as 'the death of a way of life'" (Stapley & Collie, 2004). This was a view that was expressed in fifteen different countries and provides a stunning picture of the effects of Globalization. We might reasonably ask, can anything be worse than "death of a way of life"? Judging by the most recent findings in January 2006, the answer has to be "yes".

Should anyone have doubts about the sort of effect that Globalization is having on societal cultures I wish to dispel them at this early stage. The serious nature of the current situation is captured in the following extract of a January 2006 analysis that stated:

> The world is going through a period of unprecedented and revolutionary social change that still shows no signs of relenting. The effect of Globalization has been such that it has impacted upon all aspects of society be that individuals or those responsible for the management, leadership and administration of political, economic and social institutions. Members of society in all countries are struggling to come to terms with these changes and the current social dynamics are in large part evidence of the ways that members of societies are developing means of coping. There is little if any evidence to show that any particular society has started to come to terms with a "new way of life". Indeed, the evidence is to the contrary.
>
> Changes in societies around the world are so dramatic and so destructive that individuals and groups are experiencing a loss of identity. This dire experience is described by Winnicott (1988) as, "Integration feels sane, and it feels mad to be losing integration that has been acquired"; and by Melanie Klein (1955) as, "one of the main factors underlying the need for integration is the individual's feeling that integration implies being alive, loving and being loved by the internal and external good object; that is to say, there exists a close link between integration and object-relations. Conversely the feeling of chaos, of disintegration, of lacking emotions, as a result of splitting, I take to be closely related to the fear of death." It seems little wonder therefore that members of society should describe their experience as "death of a way of life", as they did in 2004 (Stapley & Cave, 2006).

The evidence is that Globalization is exceedingly powerful and influential at both a social and a psychological level in all societies. As was stated above, messing with culture can have some serious consequences.

Structure of the book

The opening chapter, "The field of study: societal cultures", recognizes the need and provides a description and explanation of the theoretical approach taken. Extending from and expanding on the theoretical base of Group Relations learning the same ideas that are applied to the study of small and large groups is applied to society that is also seen as an intelligible field of study. The chapter describes what are considered to be the two key concepts of Group Relations learning: the notion of group-as-a-whole dynamics, and relatedness. Viewing societal dynamics from the perspective of the society-as-a-whole makes available for study dynamics of the society that are different from individual dynamics. And the concept of relatedness makes us aware of the mutual influence of individuals and groups. Having set the theoretical base this is then further extended to include societal culture that develops out of the inter-relatedness of the members of society and what is referred to as the societal holding environment that enables us to view societal dynamics as the representation of societal culture.

From here on I seek to address the main issue: that of Globalization and terrorism. In Chapter Two, "The parallel worlds of Globalization and global Muslim terrorism", the aim is to locate the study of Globalization and terrorism in an overall time scale and in a manner which enables comparative development and linkage. In this way, we can begin to gain an understanding of the way that global Muslim terrorism has developed as one of the consequences of Globalization. There are many social and political consequences of Globalization, some of which will be referred to in subsequent chapters. These should in no way be underestimated as I would suggest they will continue to have an impact on members of societies throughout the world for some considerable time. However, the current pre-occupation with what is undoubtedly the most dramatic consequence of Globalization is global Muslim terrorism.

To enable comparison of Globalization and terrorism is a difficult task as both phenomena are by their very nature ill-defined, long-term, complex processes that defy simplicity. However, by proceeding on the basis that the World Wide Web (www) was undoubtedly one of, if not the key driver and enabler, of Globalization; and that Al

Qaeda is the primary source and representation of global Muslim terrorism; we can provide the necessary picture in symbolic form. This uncanny comparison provides us with a notion of the time scale and development of both Globalization and terrorism and the way that they have developed in parallel in a simple enough way as to enable a focus that can be kept in mind. A further aim of this chapter is to provide something of a route map for what is to follow.

This is followed in Chapter Three, "The Industrial Revolution: the first Globalization", by a short and selective reference back in history to the Industrial Revolution of 1789–1848 which is now being referred to as the first Globalization or Globalization One. This chapter, in reviewing and reflecting on aspects of the historical period known as the Industrial Revolution, seeks to provide a further context for today's Globalization. There are so many important and interesting similarities in the dynamics that arose as a consequence of the Industrial Revolution and those that are currently arising as a consequence of Globalization, that it would be foolish to ignore them. The changes of the Industrial Revolution were doubtless as imperceptible then as they are now, but with the aid of hindsight they are now available as an important record. As will be shown, the depth and breadth of the changes were such that the experience then must also have been one of "death of a way of life", and the problems of adjusting to a new way of life must have been as stressful then as they are today. In addition, this period of history had such a massive impact on many societies throughout the world that it still has an enormous effect on non-Western societies today. This provides for a continuing relatedness between Western and non-Western societies and cultures that is always potentially harmful.

Chapter Four, "Globalization", brings us to the present day and begins to provide an understanding of the unprecedented and imperceptible nature of Globalization. In this chapter, I seek to provide an explanation of the way that the process of Globalization is manifesting itself in the world today. As was the experience of the Industrial Revolution, it will be shown that Globalization is not just a change in technology, but the fact that the new technology has brought into being a new way of living. Globalization, like its forerunner, was originally driven by economic need but has developed way beyond that to begin the process of creating in societies throughout the world a new way of life. The view taken here is that at this time, what that new way of life will be is not known and we are currently at the stage where we are experiencing "death of a known way of life".

In Chapter Five, "The effect of Globalization on Western societies", I shall provide the first of three analyses concerning the effects of Globalization, starting here with the effect of Globalization on Western societies. The main source for this analysis will be the findings of OPUS Listening Posts that are referred to in Chapter One. Such is the dynamic nature of the process of Globalization that the changes are largely imperceptible and the more traditional research methods are not at all helpful. A result is that other than the experience of the Industrial Revolution there really is little other material available. However, the reader will find the Listening Post material highly illuminating and a rich source of understanding.

In Chapter Six, "An analysis of the effects of Globalization on non-Western societies", the analysis continues with particular concentration on the effect of Globalization on members of Muslim societies. Sadly we do not have the rich data available as in the last analysis, instead, we have to rely on extending our thinking from a variety of sources. These include: comparison with the effects of Globalization on members of Western societies; contemporary reportage and known dynamics; and the benefit of hindsight from the experiences arising during the period of the Industrial Revolution. In this chapter and the previous one it will be seen that the consequences of the Industrial Revolution which were mainly dependency which resulted in an increased interest in evangelical religion in the West, and in the Muslim world to Islam; and violent rebellion both by members of British society and by members of societies in other countries, is being replicated today. This chapter will show that an effect of Globalization on members of Muslim societies is that of violent rebellion that manifests itself as global Muslim terrorism.

In Chapter Seven, "Exploring the effects of Globalization on inter-cultural relationships and relatedness", I will provide a concluding analysis that seeks to build on the analyses in Chapters Four and Five by exploring the effect of Globalization on inter-cultural relationships and relatedness. Exposure of the destructive affects on societal cultures enables us to think about global dynamics in a different way and one of the aims is to provide a deeper explanation of the resulting inter-cultural dynamics that are having such dangerous consequences at this time. A further aim is to encourage members of societies everywhere to understand their involvement in the processes that lead to the dangers we currently face. And most important is the vital aim of seeing the current dynamics as an inter-cultural conflict between Western societies and Muslim societies, as opposed to some smaller conflict with fundamentalist group.

How to use this book

For those who are interested in the theoretical approach taken it will be helpful to start at Chapter One. However, if you are more interested in the actuality of the subject matter it might be better to start from Chapter Two and continue through the building blocks of successive chapters that come together at the end of the book.

Acknowledgements

This book has its origins in a paper presented to a Meeting of AGSLO in Stockholm, Sweden on 2nd December 2005. I wish to express my appreciation to the Members of AGSLO for the opportunity of presenting this paper and for their warm response that encouraged the writing of this book.

I also wish to express my appreciation to Christelle Yeyet-Jacquot at Karnac for her helpful comments on an early draft and for her kindly and helpful guidance and assistance in bringing this book to fruition.

Thanks and appreciation are also due to the Conveners and many Members of OPUS Listening Posts held in different countries throughout the world who through their skill and participation have assisted in revealing that which was otherwise imperceptible.

Who is this book for?

This is a book of our time and it is likely to be of interest to those many sophisticated members of societies throughout the world who are interested in knowing more about their societies and in gaining an understanding of global Muslim terrorism. It will be particularly interesting to those reflective citizens who wish to gain a deeper understanding of their own involvement in the development of societal dynamics and societal cultures, and for those who may have the challenging task of taking the learning forward by developing multi-cultural and inter-cultural relationships in some of the most trying and difficult circumstances. For academics and students of culture it may provide some new and interesting ideas.

Not least, I would hope that it is of interest to those responsible for the management, leadership and administration of political, economic and social institutions. In particular, to politicians and those in Governments and international agencies; and that it may serve to convince them that a systems psychodynamic approach to national and inter-national affairs can provide vital new information.

GLOBALIZATION AND TERRORISM

CHAPTER ONE

The field of study: societal cultures

I n 1985 Miller and Khaleelee published a paper "Society as an intelligible field of study". In brief, this paper sought to show that society was but a (very) large group and that the same sort of theoretical understanding used in Group Relations learning where both small and large group dynamics were the subject of study in temporary institutions, could also be applied to the study of society. For those readers who are not familiar with the Group Relations approach, which is sometimes referred to as a "systems psychodynamic" approach, the short summary below is an attempt to capture the essential features. For those who may wish to obtain a more thorough understanding there are several sources available (for example see: Gould, Stapley, & Stein (2001); Gould, Stapley, & Stein (2004); Stapley (2006); Armstrong (2005) and others).

Group Relations learning

For current purposes, this short summary will provide the reader with an introduction to the main features of Group Relations learning, such as to enable a basic understanding. The purpose of Group Relations learning is educational and is devoted to experiential, or here and now, learning about group and organization behaviour. The essentials of the approach, including its theoretical underpinnings, were largely established in the 1960s. Of central theoretical and practical interest is the notion of "relatedness". That is the process of mutual influence between individual and group, group and group, group and organization, organization and organization and the relatedness of organizations and community to wider social systems including society itself. Influenced by Kurt Lewin's (1947) work, and later Bion's (1961) ground-breaking findings about group dynamics, the importance of studying the group-as-a-whole was considered paramount. Other psychoanalytic concepts, such as those of Melanie Klein (1959), were later found to be invaluable in understanding group dynamics. Psychoanalysis, besides suggesting that explanations for human behaviour in groups may be found in primitive and unconscious processes, also provided a model for working with groups and organizations. A key concept also derived from Lewin (1935) and developed by open system theorists was that of "boundary". This was seen as significant in terms of any defined system, be that the task, an individual, a group, an organization, or society. (See Miller (1989) for a fuller description of Group Relations development and processes.)

From the above it will be appreciated why the theoretical underpinning resulted in it being referred to as systems psychodynamics. It includes psychoanalytic concepts that are social and psychological in nature but in addition moves from individual dynamics to a group-as-a-whole or systemic perspective. Seen in this light, the group (organization or society) can be conceptualized as behaving in a different manner from but related to the dynamics of the members; and, from this vantage point groups-as-a-whole have their own dynamics resulting from the interactions of group members who are interdependent members and sub-systems.

Margaret Thatcher, when Prime Minister of Great Britain, famously stated that, "there was no such thing as society". Her point being that society was made up of individuals and only individuals were responsible for what occurred. If, as will be shown below, she had been trained in a systems psychodynamic way she might have come to a different conclusion. The very substance of the object relations argument in psychoanalysis is that the dominating feature of human psychology is an impulse to form relationships—a social orientation. For Melanie Klein (1975) human drives are emotions directed towards others, real or imaginary, from the beginning of life: drives are relationships. Thus throughout our lives we are constantly in a system of relatedness with others. As will be seen, this is an important notion. By relatedness I mean the mutual influence that societies and cultures have on each other at many levels. The mutual influence may sometimes be influenced by events many years in the past and are vital to our understanding of current day events.

To appreciate the systems psychodynamic approach it is important to have an understanding of two essential elements of Group Relations learning: those of relatedness (referred to above) and the group-as-a-whole. We will all be familiar with frequent references to the notion of a group or societal mind or of groups behaving as an organism. Indeed, it is not uncommon for some to erroneously speak of organizations or societies as actively doing something or other. But, we may ask, how can this be? We know that only individuals have minds and that no such thing as a group mind exists. It is individual human beings who are constantly engaged in the process of meaning making. And it is only the functioning of individual minds that make the human collectively possible. Without human minds, neither language, nor culture nor rules could exist. How or why, then, do we develop the idea that a "group mind" exists?

What we can say is that groups act "as if" they have a group mind: that the group is a construct and that without individual human activity the construct of the group-as-a-whole simply would not exist. The group is to be seen as an artificial creation, it is a mental construct. A mental construct that is hypothesized to come about from our human need to belong and to establish a state of psychological unity with others which represents a covert wish for restoring an earlier state of unconflicted well-being inherent in the exclusive union with mother. Put another way, we seek to recreate in the present a holding environment that will provide us with the same sort of psychological and social support that we experienced in the maternal holding environment. We need the group to provide us with a favourable emotional response as much as we needed mother to do so. And this is usefully added to by Bion's (1961) notion of "groupishness", a proclivity to and need to be members of groups. A measure of the importance that the group has for us is perhaps illustrated by the way we quickly come to identify with a group. (For a fuller discussion of group-as-a-whole see Stapley, 2006).

Working from this theoretical base, our primary focus in groups (including society) needs to be the group-as-a-whole and this includes what individuals or sub-groups may do. Roles that are taken up by group members are to be seen as a function of the group-as-a-whole and the behaviour of a person in a group has more to do with the group than it does with his or her individuality. I should stress that I am not here referring to formal, allocated roles. What I am referring to are roles that members of a group unconsciously take on as a result of beneath the surface processes. Thus, any role taken by an individual member of a group may be considered to be a group role, one that is a function of group dynamics. When role is defined as a property of the group, then role prescriptions are filled, sometimes by individuals, sometimes by sub-groups and sometimes by identifiable clusters of behaviour that are a group property and serve a role function, although they appear independent from all individual members or sub-groups. These group or societal role dynamics are to be seen as a manifestation of the group or society-as-a-whole.

Society as a large group

As members of a society we are still part of a group, and the same theoretical and practical findings associated with Group Relations learning can be applied to society. There is much evidence to suggest that as in smaller groups so also in societal groups, various individuals but mainly groups are motivated to act on behalf of their societal 'group'. Thus we may see Trade Unions mobilized to lead the fight against perceived social injustice at work. Or a group of entertainers may be mobilized to lead the fight against perceived injustice and starvation in a foreign country. And a group of anti-war protesters may be mobilized to fight against the perceived wrongness of war and aggression. Or as was recently the case in America, where a large group of some million people who seemingly came out of nowhere, having been both consciously and unconsciously mobilized to demonstrate for immigrant rights. But to really understand the dynamics occurring at the time of these events we need to take our analysis further. In all these and similar situations we need to ask what the societal sub-group is doing on behalf of society as a whole. What is the underlying anxiety experienced by members of society to which they are reacting?

Unlike smaller groups where we can more easily identify the boundaries, society is a much more complicated group and lacking clear boundaries. This, I believe, is a major contributory factor that acts to inhibit thoughts about society and one of the reasons for the imperceptible nature of change. Society is, of course, less a finished product than a transitive process. While it has some stable features, it is at the same time continually undergoing change. A result is that "society" is a term frequently used as a sort of "cover all" for all sorts of explanations. It is as if society is simply there as a matter of fact requiring no further explanation. This is very similar to "societal culture" which is a phenomenon that can be regarded in the same way as society and one that, it is suggested, cannot be avoided when considering society.

Societal culture

Studying societies as societies, which is societies studied from a group-as-a-whole perspective, leads us to add to Miller and Khaleelee's thinking to include the notion of societal culture. As is the case with regard to the term "society", the term "culture" has been in common usage for many years and is a familiar notion. Unfortunately, this common usage has itself led to problems. For example, cultural differences are seen as being in the nature of things requiring no explanation. A result is that functions that are not easily understood are assigned to a mysterious central agency called "culture" accompanied by a declaration that "it" performs in a particular way. Culture is also an easy option to fall back on to solve all our unexplained problems. In addition, past uses of the word to designate a way of life such as a particular society, or part of a society, are exceedingly vague.

However, as vague as our understanding of culture may be, it is also vital to our understanding of different societies and in particular to our understanding of cross-cultural relationships. I shall start with a clarification of what is meant by culture using my previously developed work (Stapley, 1996) to provide an explanation for the way that cultures develop. I am taking as a given that there are a multitude of different cultures and sub-cultures, both societal and organizational. I shall not, therefore, relate to any particular culture but will provide a general theory that can be applied to any society or organization.

Societal culture is a complicated yet highly influential phenomenon and the degree of complication is likely to be much greater in a situation where multiple societal cultures prevail. I would suggest that in the past we have been more concerned with identifying the nature or the symptoms of a culture rather than understanding what it is. My approach seeks to provide an answer to that most fundamental of questions: that concerning how culture develops, working from the principle that if we know how it develops we shall be able to unpack it and therefore know how to influence it. In other words, knowing how culture develops will provide us with an understanding of the causes of the consistent behaviour that we call culture.

We can say that culture develops out of the interrelatedness of the members of a society and the societal holding environment. The external and internal worlds of members of societies are in continual interaction: what goes on in the minds of members of societies is partly reactive to what happens around them, but is also very much proactive. The ideas and ways of thinking of members of societies influence the way they act upon their surroundings to bring about change in them. In this way we can develop the understanding that culture is in the individual and that the individual is in the culture. The constant interaction between the individual and culture is fundamental to any study of culture, or for that matter, personality. They are indivisibly linked and consequently it is helpful to bear in mind both processes.

The influences which culture exerts on the developing personality are of two quite different sorts. On the one hand, we have those influences that derive from the culturally patterned behaviour of individuals towards the child. These begin to operate from the moment of birth, a matter that will shortly be dealt with in greater detail. On the other hand, we have those influences that derive from the individual's observation of, or instruction in, the patterns of behaviour characteristic of their society. The fact that personality norms differ in different societies can be explained on the basis of the different experiences that the members of such societies acquire from contact with those societies. However, what we need to study is the processes of these societal experiences.

Every society consists of individuals developing from children into parents. In the earliest days the mother provides the context in which development takes place, and from the point of view of the newborn she is part of the self. She provides a true psycho-social context: she is both "psycho" and "social" depending on whose perspective we take, and the transformation by which she becomes for the infant gradually less "psycho" and more "social" describes the very evolution of meaning itself. In Winnicott's (1971) view, what he refers to as the "holding environment" is vital to the development of the infant. From the beginning of life, reliable holding has to be a feature of the environment if the child is to survive.

The notion of a "holding environment" is seen as the key concept in providing an explanation of how culture develops. Holding in the mother's womb and then holding in the mother's arms, is the first boundary out of chaos within which the infant's personality can develop. The early relation in the maternal holding environment is characterized by infantile dependence, that is, a dependence based on a primary identification with the object, and an inability to differentiate and adapt. A relationship grows through the ability of both parties to experience and adjust to each other's natures. The relationship develops through the infant getting to know the mother as she presents herself to interpret and meet his needs, which are emotional as well as physical. For the infant to develop there is a need for a "basic trust" in the maternal holding environment and for what Winnicott (1971) has referred to as "a good enough holding environment".

As the infant grows there develops the formation of a self-concept. This psychological change arises once the infant is able to experience the mother and other significant objects as separate. Gradually there develop several "not me's" in the shape of father, siblings, playmates and other relations. At this stage the infant is capable of introjecting cognitive symbols. And here the holding environment begins to split into an internalized psychological part and an external social part. By "taking in" (introjecting), "summoning up" and "holding in mind" their perceptions as if they were an object, infants feel that they contain within themselves a world of concrete things of at least as much reality as the material world.

Early introjections (taking in of external objects), since they are virtually all the infant has, are particularly potent, and the inner "objects" (the mental images) they create are never forgotten. These early introjections, which of necessity are of parents or parental figures, create an inner object commonly referred to as the conscience or in technical term the superego. The introjection of the "good" parent creates what I shall refer to as the ideal conscience, that is, a sense of ideals and positive morality—a pattern of what to do. And introjection of the "bad" parent creates what I shall refer to as the persecutory conscience, a sense of guilt and negative morality—of what not to do. Conscience, then, is built up by identifying with, that is forming and taking in and retaining, mental images of parental figures. It is realized that these images are not built on the reality of parents' behaviour, but on the way that the infant perceives reality— which of course may be total phantasy. Thus the reality may have been that the parent was very caring, but that his or her behaviour was perceived as uncaring by the infant. Introjection is a very important concept, which simply involves the creation of an internal object that may be another person, a quality of another person, or a concept, and may include family and societal values.

To summarize, the "maternal holding environment" consists first of the mother and child and later the father and other important relatives. In this "holding environment" there is a continuing inter-relationship between the mother and the child. The mother influences the child and the child influences the mother. In other words the child is part of the "holding environment" and influences it while at the same time the child is influenced by the "holding environment". The development of the personality of the child will depend upon whether the holding environment has been "good enough". As the infant grows, he or she becomes a member of several holding environments: the family, the school, the university, the organization or work, and the societal holding environments. Indeed, I will go further than this because I believe it is more accurate to state that there is not only a succession of "holding environments" but that several "holding environments" may be available for any one individual at any given time. This may be especially so regarding societal, work and family holding environments which we will all influence and at the same time be influenced by.

As was mentioned above, our experience of the maternal holding environment has a lasting effect and we subsequently seek to recreate in the present day group a holding environment that will provide us with the sort of psychological and social support that we experienced in the maternal holding environment. Perhaps not surprisingly the societal (or organizational) holding environment consists of both a social or external part and a psychological or internal part. These two levels are in constant interaction: what goes on in the minds of members of a society is partly a reaction to what goes on around them in the external holding environment but is also very much pro-active. Members of societies ideas and their ways of thinking—the internal holding environment—influences the way that members of a society act upon their external holding environment to bring about change. Seen from the added perspective of society-as-a-whole the result is the way things are done around here, or societal culture.

Having demonstrated the importance of the maternal holding environment in the process of personality development, I shall now develop the concept of a "societal holding environment". In much the same way that we interrelate with the maternal holding environment, so we interrelate with the societal holding environment. We use it to supply the same needs as the maternal holding environment and we apply the same affect to it and create similar defences when it is seen as "not good enough". There is never total independence, the healthy individual does not become isolated, but continues to be related to the environment in such a way that the individual and the environment can be said to be interdependent. In much the same way as there is a need for a "basic trust" in the maternal holding environment and for what Winnicott termed a "good enough holding environment" if the infant is to develop, so there is a similar need here in the societal holding environment. As with the mother, such "basic trust" is developed as a result of the perceived experience of the societal holding environment by the members of the society.

In the same way that unconscious forces operate in the maternal holding environment so they are also at play here in the societal holding environment. Consequently, it is not only helpful but also necessary to view the societal holding environment as consisting of two parts. In this respect, the "iceberg" analogy previously used by other writers to describe culture may be a useful way of viewing things. The physical or sociological part of the holding environment is that part which is exposed or is conscious. This is *the external holding environment* which consists of: the formal structures and strategies of those responsible for the management, leadership and administration of political, economic and social institutions; the roles of members; all forms of knowledge and skills; and values and attitudes shared by the members. The psychological part of the holding environment is internalized and largely unconscious. This is *the internalized holding environment* that consists of the internal objects which are regarded as part of the self and compose the basic social character of the individual.

As stated earlier, culture develops out of the interrelatedness of the members of the society and the societal holding environment. The societal holding environment consists of the totality of the society including the members of the society themselves. The specific societal holding environment provides the context in which development of culture takes place. However, there are various aspects within that totality that will have a particular influence on the members' perceived notion of the society. In the maternal holding environment, the particular influence was the mother and later the father and other important relatives. In the societal holding environment it may be political, religious or other significant social figures; in others it may be the provision (or lack of) containment, or even a lack of basic matters such as food and shelter. In this respect, I think there is value in applying Maslow's hierarchy of needs. So that when basic needs are fulfilled other higher level needs affect our view of the societal holding environment.

It is suggested that the representation of society—"the way things are done around here"—and what we are in effect referring to when we speak of societal dynamics is in fact "societal culture". Societal culture (as is organizational culture) is something that a society "is". As opposed to a notion that culture is something that exists as a separate entity: something that an organization "has". This is an important point because viewing culture as something that a society "is" leads us to the notion that culture is within all of us who are members of a particular society. We ultimately comprise society and societal culture and in effect we are societal culture. We may, then, conclude that societal dynamics are synonymous with societal cultures; they are the way things are done around here.

The various identities that we take will affect our perceptive filters, as will the holding environments that we are a part of. So that, based on current and past experience, conscious and unconscious processes, the internalized multiple experiences result in a construct that we may refer to as "the society in the mind". It is this construct of a society in the mind that members of society interrelate with. And the way that the members of the society perceive the "society in the mind" will determine the culture. It will depend whether or not there is a "basic trust" and whether the holding environment is viewed as "good enough". The behaviour adopted by the members of the society will depend upon their psychological perception of the societal holding environment, or, their view of the "society in their minds". Whatever their view, members of the society will adopt forms of behaviour that they feel are appropriate to them under the circumstances that they perceive are imposed upon them by their holding environment. The end result is consistent forms of behaviour that have previously been defined as "the way things are done around here".

Characteristics of culture

Defining, describing, and understanding societal culture is indeed difficult. But difficult as it may be we can say that societal (or organizational) culture is characterized by the following:

1. It is a psycho-social process;
2. It is evidenced by sameness and continuity to provide for the self-esteem of the members and their sense of reality with others;
3. Being a psychological as well as a social process it is influenced by conscious and unconscious processes;
4. Both the uniqueness of the collective, perceived view of the

members of the society and the societal holding environment results in a unique culture in every society and part of a society;

5. Because groups are ongoing structures as opposed to finished ones, it is a dynamic and changing process;

6. The members of a group, organization or society will produce forms of behaviour which they consider will be psychologically advantageous to them under the conditions they perceive are imposed on them by the environment.

For current purposes, it will be seen that two of the characteristics of culture are seemingly contradictory. Societal culture is at one and the same time "evidenced by sameness and continuity" and "a dynamic and changing process". This is important to an under-standing of current societal dynamics. About ten or more years ago, societal cultures around the world would have been strongly evi-denced by "sameness and continuity". The "dynamic processes" would have been few and far between and would have been taken in their stride by members of societies. However in the last decade, and especially in the last four or five years, the "dynamic processes" have become progressively more apparent and have had a huge influence on societies. A result is that continuity and sameness are almost non-existent at this time. This in turn creates a situation that leads to a loss of containment and of identity as was referred to in the Preface.

Societal culture may be viewed from different but linked levels. At the macro level we might refer to Western culture that encompasses those parts of the world that share a Western political, social and economic philosophy. At a lower level we might refer to American, Chinese, Swedish or British societal culture and below that we might even refer to a regional societal culture. And beyond that we might consider organizational culture. The latter raises an interesting point when we consider the effects of the culture of Multi-National Com-panies on National and Western societal culture and perhaps more importantly on non-Western societal cultures.

The foregoing has not only provided something of the theoretical approach but has also provided the reader with something of the complexity of the field of study. In the Preface I referred to the unprecedented and imperceptible nature of Globalization when viewed from the perspective of contemporary analysis. As such, you may agree that most existing methodologies are quite inadequate to provide us with explanations and understanding of current dynamics in society. However, a unique practical application of the theoretical approach described, which is based on the theory and practice of Group Relations learning, has been developed by OPUS over the past twenty-five years. It is this methodology and other experiential learning groups that OPUS bring to this important area of research which makes possible the exploration of societal dynamics as an identifiable field of study.

OPUS methodology

The methodology is referred to as OPUS Listening Posts that enable us to explore societies as societies and to expose and explore beneath the surface experiences in societies so that we can analyse and develop hypotheses that will account for what we don't understand. The aim of Listening Posts is to enable participants as individual citizens to reflect on their own relatedness to society and to try to develop an understanding of what is happening in society at any given moment. Listening Posts provide an opportunity for participants to share their preoccupations in relation to the various societal roles they may have. And collectively they are invited to try to identify the underlying dynamics, both conscious and unconscious, that may be predominant at the time.

Listening Posts are based on the notion that a group of people meeting together to study the behaviour of the society as a society allows the unconscious expression of some characteristics of the wider social system, and the experience of the Listening Post is itself, therefore, relevant to an understanding of society beyond individual and personal preoccupations. This is important and unique work that provides valuable data about current dynamics in society at any given time. By using a group of citizens to explore their own preoccupations and experiences of society we can use the group as a sort of sounding board to reveal the current state of society that can then, with the help of a skilled convener, be self-analysed to produce hypotheses that are explanations for what was previously not understood

Listening Posts provide the opportunity for members to share their preoccupations and experiences as free flowing raw data, unprovoked, unsolicited, unguided and unfocused. In doing so, they provide us with a direct contact with the societal culture. This approach is rather like sticking a probe into something and taking a sample for analysis. What this sample reveals is totally different in quality from that of other forms of research. It is an insight into the ideas and ways of thinking of people that both determine how members of societies perceive the external realities and shape their actions towards them. They include their beliefs and values, their hopes, anxieties, and various defence mechanisms that they may employ. From the resulting analyses we are able to provide hypotheses that are explanations for what we previously did not understand about any particular society.

A regular Listening Post is held in London on a quarterly basis and irregularly at other locations throughout Britain. In addition, for the past three years OPUS has also run an International Listening Post Project. In 2004 thirteen countries were involved in this Project; in 2005 fifteen countries; and in 2006 twenty-two countries. This particular Project results in a Global Dynamics Report. The outcome of all Listening Posts is a Report that provides an analysis and hypotheses about current dynamics in society. Further references will be made to the findings of Listening Posts throughout the book, particularly in Chapter Five. But having set the theoretical scene I now want to set the practical scene by using the next chapter to first locate the issue of Globalization and terrorism in a context and time frame that shows how Muslim and Western cultures have collided at the interface, one of the results being global Muslim terrorism. In doing so I shall provide an outline of the development of the World Wide Web and of Al Qaeda that are seen as symbolic representations of both Globalization and terrorism. It will also provide a sort of route map that will provide a starting point for the main argument that I am putting forward in this book, namely, the notion that Globalization and global Muslim terrorism have developed in parallel—the latter being a consequence to the former.

CHAPTER TWO

The parallel worlds of Globalization and global Muslim terrorism

This book seeks to provide an insight to the unprecedented and imperceptible changes that are arising as part of the processes of Globalization. In particular, it will focus on the consequences of Globalization: the way that a rational, economic process impacts on societal cultures throughout the world. The central thesis of this book is that a consequence of Western Globalization has been such as to have largely destroyed the sameness and continuity of societal cultures across the world. And this is experienced by members in both Western and non-Western societies as death of a way of life leading to a loss of identity. Faced with such unbearable experiences members of societies are unable to make sense of their environment. They respond to this experience in various ways but there are two particular responses that are constantly present in all societies. The first is dependency, which may hardly be a surprise. But more interestingly the nature of the dependency is highly primitive and is in the nature of a search for a Messiah or saviour. For large numbers of Western societies the object of their dependency needs is evangelical religion; while in Muslim societies nearly everyone turns to Islam, as an object of their dependency needs. The other particular response is through violent rebellion. In Western societies we see young people rioting in the streets; in Muslim societies we see suicide bombers and others engaged in global terrorism.

As was explained in the last chapter, the approach taken is to view societies-as-a-whole, whereby the field of study is concerned with looking at a society as a society and that acts done by individuals or sub-groups of society are regarded as acts done on behalf of that society. Put another way such acts are part of a societal dynamic and are not seen as individual actions. In taking this approach we can begin to view the current societal dynamics in a different manner: one that enables us to gain a deeper understanding of what is undoubtedly a dangerous situation. Thus the view taken here is that Al Qaeda or other Muslim terrorist groups are doing something on behalf of Muslim societies. And of course this also applies to acts committed by individuals and groups in Western societies. In this book the notion that Al Qaeda and others are simply a small group of global Muslim terrorists is rejected. For politicians and perhaps members of Western societies it may be an anxiety-reducing notion to consider that the problem is able to be managed by seeing the problem in a small compartmentalized manner, but this is to ignore the true source of the problem which is a serious and disturbing conflict at the boundary between Muslim and Western cultures. Understanding the important notion that terrorism committed by Al Qaeda is something done on behalf of Muslim societies identifies the source of the problem. And this leads to the ultimate purpose of the book that is to explore some of the issues concerning the development of inter-cultural relationships.

In this chapter I want to set the scene for what will follow in subsequent chapters which are intended to take the discussion and exploration further until we are in a position in the concluding chapter to achieve the ultimate aim referred to above. At the centre of this exploration is the process that we call Globalization which, it is suggested, has created societal dynamics such as to make this a most complex and complicated period of our history. Even though the changes have been and continue to be in the nature of a revolution, for most of us the continuance and profundity of change makes it nigh impossible to keep pace with what is happening. We, and members of societies throughout the world, are part of these changes. It is "us", our culture, that is being torn apart, and we are frequently overwhelmed by the emotions aroused. It's rather like being in the middle of a constant and continuing fight where it's impossible to think and reflect. It's as much as we can do to concentrate on the current situation and to work out how to survive in the world at any given moment. But that should not detract from the extreme nature of the changes that are a consequence of Globalization and which are affecting members of societies throughout the world in equally extreme ways, as will be shown throughout the book.

I don't use the term "revolution" lightly, but on any scale this is a period of history that is changing our very way of life. If it were an earthquake we were studying it would be rated exceedingly high on the Richter scale. Or to use the terminology of Thomas Kuhn (1962) it is a point where we are living through a Paradigm change: a point where the old way of thinking and behaving is no longer valid and helpful. A period in time when we are developing a new Paradigm: a new way of life. At this point we do not know the nature of the new Paradigm as we are still experiencing the death of a known way of life. How things will develop we cannot say at this time. However, as difficult as the task of understanding may be, such are the consequences that the need for understanding is paramount if we are to develop peaceful inter-cultural relations. I have described above just how difficult it is for members of society to go beyond something other than a general impression that they are in the process of profound societal change. There is the added problem that psychological and unconscious processes are also evoked by the extreme anxiety arising from the current dynamics: these can and do result in polarization leading to conflictual inter-cultural relations.

Before getting involved in the more detailed discussions that will support the main purpose of this book, I want to explore something of the way that Western and Muslim cultures have collided and created an abrasive and dangerous interface: one where Globalization leads to global Muslim terrorism. This is largely the story of the way that Western Globalization, coming on top of what was an already existing lack of trust in and fear of domination by the West, has greatly increased the fears and anxieties of members of Muslim societies. And this has in turn threatened their individual and group identity and raised their dependency needs whereby they have turned to Islam. A problem is that Islamic leaders also feel that their identity is threatened by the advances of Globalization. We therefore have a combination of factors; high dependency on Islam and Islamic leaders who respond with violent aggression towards those who would attempt to change their way of life. With religious leaders behaving in this way it can only result in members of Muslim societies acting in the same manner. A result is that aggressive violence against the West becomes part of Muslim culture: it is the way of life for members of Muslim societies. This then leads to individuals and groups being unconsciously mobilized to act on behalf of Muslim society to carry out acts of aggressive violence against the West. Thus we have Osama Bin Laden, Al Quaeda and other Muslim terrorists who are engaged in global terrorism.

Muslim terrorism is, on several dimensions, of a different nature to that of other terrorism. Prior to the recent Muslim atrocities, acts of terrorism were mainly either intra-national such as the acts of terror committed by the IRA in the United Kingdom, by ETA in Spain, or by the Tamil Tigers in Sri Lanka, or they were acts committed by terrorist groups against foreign interests in their own societies. Muslim terrorism is a new phenomenon, it is inter-cultural and it is global in nature. It is also at a different level whereby those concerned commit acts of terrorism that are of an unprecedented degree of violence. A measure of the unprecedented nature of global Muslim terrorism is the way that Western security services were totally unaware of the threat. The resultant wringing of hands by governments and security services after the atrocity on 9/11 and subsequent atrocities around the world, serves to show that there was little if any belief of such a threat even to the extent that valuable evidence that was available was ignored. It is possible that the absence of a society-as-a-whole perspective helped to bring about this result.

Globalization has had serious consequences for all societies, Western and non-Western alike, and I do not want to ignore the dire effect of Globalization on every other society but there are various reasons that we need to understand why Globalization should have a more profound effect on Muslim society than on other societies throughout the world. Exploring the context enables us to consider that even before Globalization began its seemingly inexorable intrusion into and destruction of the societal cultures of the world, relationships between Muslim and Western societies were never amicable. Each society had a distinctly different culture that was a very different way of life. Other than the important fact that both we and they are all human beings, the way we and they live our lives is markedly different. This may be true of other cultures such as Chinese culture but it is not to the same degree and there are other factors that affect Muslim societies. For example, they are economically and militarily weak compared with some other non-Western societies. Muslim or Islamic society is part of many nations and does not have a specific national voice to provide a political response. And it is not wealthy enough to provide a copy-cat economic response such as that of the South Americans and Chinese. This really leaves them with few options and the response of Muslim or Islamic societies is to aggressively reject Western values and attempts to impose a Western way of life on them.

Over the years, Western know-how, economic and military clout ensured that the West controlled oil production that was the main source of revenue for most Muslim societies. But this was more of a "working arrangement" than a relationship between Muslims and the West. Even while this working arrangement was in place several Muslim societies were engaged in constant anti-Western activities. And, most of the Muslim world is committed to the destruction of (Western) Israel. Seen from a systemic perspective we can view the interface between Israel and the Muslim world as a microcosm of that between Muslim and Western cultures. Put another way, Israel is to be seen as a symbolic representation of Western societies. Thus we see the hatred and the violence that Muslims have for the West being displaced onto Israel. From this perspective we should be under no illusions about the feelings of members of Muslim societies for "us" in the West. Taking this notion further we might also wish to consider that the Iranian view that Israel should be wiped off the map is Iran doing something on behalf of Muslim society.

Thus we can see that a combination of Globalization that has the effect of seeking to impose a new way of life on Muslim societies and a Muslim society that has traditionally found all things Western as abhorrent to their way of life combine to produce a highly threatening and chaotic situation whereby members of Muslim societies seek for relief from the severe threats they are experiencing. Although they could control oil production that would damage the West, unlike other non-Western societies they are relatively economically weak. They are also militarily weak and such military that they do have is in the control of various Muslim societies. From this point we might try to put ourselves in the shoes of Muslim leaders. By Muslim leaders, I of course refer to Islamic leaders, because unlike Western secular states Muslim society is to a great extent controlled by Islam. Faced with such an intrusion into their way of life it might not be surprising if they responded by saying something like "they will not change our way of life". For the most part though they will doubtless experience the situation as helpless and hopeless and from this position will become even more angry and frustrated to the extent that they may consider extreme measures to preserve their way of life.

From this point it is a relatively short step from the angry tirades of the clerics, who are to be seen as doing something on behalf of the Muslim society, to the global terrorism that has ensued. We in the West are inclined to ignore those matters that don't sit easily with our understanding. When this happens we stereotype, for example "the mad Mullahs" and the "barbaric killers". But, difficult as it may be, we would be better advised, to listen carefully and to try to understand what is being said both by the suicide bombers and by the Clerics. What they say is said on behalf of members of Muslim societies. To listen is to begin to understand; to ignore is to perpetuate the inter-cultural clash. I should add that this message equally applies to members of Muslim societies who are also inclined to ignore those matters that do not sit easily with their understanding. Thus here we are, Muslim societies fighting to preserve their way of life as a result of the effects of Globalization and responding by committing acts of global terrorism against the West; and Western societies fighting to preserve their way of life against those acts of terror and responding by an attack on Iraq, an intrusion in Afghanistan, and a war on terror. And that is where we are at this time in some sort of inescapable vortex.

In the last few pages I have tried to convey the way that Globalization and terrorism are indivisibly linked and the way that a consequence of Globalization coming on top of previous experiences of Western societies has resulted in Muslim societies responding through the use of global terrorism. To shed further light on the complexity of Globalization and in particular its consequences on Muslim societies I shall use a variety of sources. One of those sources is the period of history known as the Industrial Revolution.

In Chapter Three I will show that there are several benefits to be gained from this source which was a period that had many similarities and consequences, and we are fortunate that we now have the benefit of hindsight which enables us to gain a deeper understanding of the present. From this historical perspective I move forward in Chapter Four to an exploration of Globalization with a view to trying to understand the nature of the processes and the political and economic intentions behind those processes. In Chapters Five and Six I seek to show the effect of Globalization, first on Western societies and secondly on non-Western societies. These chapters lead to a final chapter that is concerned with exploring some of the issues concerning the development of inter-cultural relationships.

By way of further introduction the following discussion on the way that Globalization and global Muslim terrorism have developed in parallel will provide an opportunity to locate the study of Globalization and terrorism in an overall time scale and in a manner which enables comparative development and linkage. In this way, we can gain a further level of understanding of the way that global Muslim terrorism has developed as one of the consequences of Globalization. The process I will use is to rely upon the development of the World Wide Web (www) and the development of Al Qaeda as symbolic representations of the development of both Globalization and global Muslim terrorism respectively. As was described above, with the advent of Globalization there developed Al Qaeda as a global Muslim terrorist organization. From media reports and other public records it is possible to trace the beginnings and activities of Osama Bin Laden and Al Qaeda which enables us to track progress over a period of time. The significance of Al Qaeda is that they are to be seen as the main Muslim global terrorist group who have been mobilized to fight by Muslim society. In other words, they were and are to be seen as doing something on behalf of Muslim society.

It is a difficult and complicated task to trace the beginnings and activities of Globalization. However, we can work on the basis that the World Wide Web (www) was such a substantial element in the development of Globalization that by tracking the development of the www and other associated developments we can achieve a fairly accurate record of the progress over a period of time. In this respect, Tom Forester, in a book titled *The Information Technology Revolution* published in 1985, predicted that the future was going to see a period of very rapid change in technology, to such an extent that there was talk of another Industrial Revolution. He also suggested that the coming changes would be based on the computer, on telecommunications and on the power that they give us over the manipulation of information. Perhaps even more significant than what he says is what he does not say: he made no mention of Globalization or the www whatever.

In 1993 Daniel Burrus, in a book called *Technotrends*, did refer to Globalization when he stated that technology alters reality. His view was that without advanced technology there would be no Globalization, and that we would not have the capability to manage the decentralization of power and authority. He stated that without the technology, global demographic changes would be greatly limited. For Burrus technological innovations therefore represented the enabling change agent. What had of course changed between 1985 and 1993 was the introduction of the World Wide Web, the main technological enabler and driver of Globalization. The development of the www should be seen in the context of previous developments regarding electronic communication (email). However, it is suggested that without and until the www was available the rate of progress and development of Globalization was nowhere near as significant as after it became available.

By concentrating, in a symbolic manner, on the development of the www and the rise of Al Qaeda we are able to begin to appreciate the way that Globalization and terrorism have developed in a parallel manner. The two short histories of the www and Al Qaeda in the following chart are chronological records of developments. They are not intended to be detailed records, rather they are intended to be a concise record that will enable the reader to easily compare one against the other. The intention is to show a time line.

Development of the World Wide Web (www) and the growth of Al Qaeda: a comparison

	A Short History of the World Wide Web	*A Short History of Al Qaeda*
1980	Prior to 1980 the internet was gradually beginning to take shape and this starts to develop at a rapid pace during the 1980s.	
	Tim Berners-Lee (the acknowledged creator of the www), while consulting for the Conseil Européen pour la Recherche Nucléaire (CERN), writes a notebook program called "Enquire-Within-Upon-Every-thing" which allows links to be made between arbitrary nodes. Each node has a title, a type, and a list of bidirectional typed links.	
1982	Development is aided by the launch of the first personal computers by IBM, which also spreads rapidly for offices and home usage.	
1984	The Domain Name system is introduced.	Osama Bin Laden starts an international body in Afghanistan which he calls "The Office of Service". At about this time he declares a Holy War or Jihad against Jews and Christians.
1986		Bin Laden is actively engaged in the war against the Soviet Union in Afghanistan and is supplied with Stinger missiles courtesy of the CIA. It will be noted that he is already being mobilized by Muslim society to fight against those seen as acting against Muslim interests.
		By this time Bin Laden is already thinking and acting globally and is estimated to have had branches in 35 countries.

Continued overleaf

	A Short History of the World Wide Web	*A Short History of Al Qaeda*
1988		Russia is forced to withdraw from Afghanistan. This is the first time in modern history that a superpower had been defeated by a non-nuclear enemy. Bin Laden is seen as a hero by others in the Muslim world.
		By now, Al Qaeda has been clearly established and is positioned firmly against the USA.
1989	(March) Tim Berners-Lee takes his thinking forward when he writes and circulates at CERN a paper entitled "Information Management: A Proposal" seeking comments.	
	(October) Tim starts work on a hypertext browser and editor. At this historic moment he makes up "World Wide Web" as a name for the program.	
	(November), Tim Berners-Lee gives a colloquium on hypertext in general. By Christmas of 1989, a line mode browser and WorldWideWeb browser/editor are able to be demonstrated. Access is possible to hypertext files, CERNVM "FIND", and Internet news articles.	
1991	(February/March) A presentation of the project is made to the ECP/PT group; a line mode browser (www) is released to a limited audience on "priam" vax.	Largely as a result of his threats Bin Laden, a Saudi national, has to move out of Saudi Arabia and he moves his organization and headquarters to the Sudan.
	(May) A work plan is produced for the CN/AS group; a presentation is made to the "C5" Committee; and there is a general release of www on central CERN machines.	
	(12 June) There is a CERN Computer Seminar on www.	

On 12th December, the first Web server outside of Europe is installed at SLAC.

1992   Throughout the year further significant developments continue including several test versions of www in various organizations.

Bin Laden and Al Qaeda are operating on a global basis and during the year, Yusuf—one of those who would be involved in the World Trade Center bombing—attends a bomb-making course in Pakistan. By this stage Al Qaeda has started planning for the World Trade Center bombing. The choice of target is, by its very nature, closely and readily related to Globalization.
overleaf

1993   Early in the year, developments continue and others are joining the project.

(30th April) CERN's directors make a declaration that www technology will be freely usable by anyone, with no fees being payable to CERN. This is regarded as a milestone document.

(July) From hereon, things begin to move at a pace. Ari Luotonen (ECP) joins the project at CERN. He implements access authorization and proceeds to re-write the CERN httpd server.

(September) NCSA releases working versions of Mosaic browser for all common platforms: X, PC/Windows and Macintosh.

(October) There are now over 200 known HTTP servers. The European Commission, the Fraunhofer Gesellschaft and CERN start the first Web-based project of the European Union, using the Web for dissemination of technological information to Europe's less favoured regions.

(February) The bombing of the underground car park of the World Trade Center in New York kills six people and wounds a further thousand people.

Continued

	A Short History of the World Wide Web	A Short History of Al Qaeda
	(December) John Markov writes a page and a half on www and Mosaic in *The New York Times'* (US) Business Section; *Guardian* (UK) publishes a page on www; *The Economist* (UK) analyses the Internet and www.	
1994	(January) O'Reilly, Spry, etc. announce "Internet in a box" product to bring the Web into homes.	(July) Bin Laden in Pakistan and a $2M reward is offered for the capture of Yusuf.
	(25th–27th May) The First International www Conference, CERN, Geneva. Heavily oversubscribed (800 apply, 400 allowed in).	Around this time, the 9/11 plane hijackers Atta and Muraili come on the scene and embrace Islam.
	(June) M. Bangemann present his Report on European Commission Information Superhighway plan. By now there are over 1500 registered servers. And the load on the first Web server is 1000 times what it had been 3 years earlier.	Later in the year, Osama Bin Laden is still having to operate from the Sudan, from where he funds the headquarters for Al Qaeda. At this stage, the CIA start to pick up intelligence about, and subsequently identify, Osama Bin Laden as a terrorist threat. Throughout this time he develops and runs training camps for Muslim terrorists.
	(September) The European Commission and CERN propose the WebCore project for development of the Web core technology in Europe.	
	(1st October) The World Wide Web Consortium is founded.	
	(December) The first W3 Consortium Meeting takes place at MIT in Cambridge, Mass. (USA); and the first meeting with European Industry and the European Consortium branch, at the European Commission in Brussels.	

1995

By this stage the www is becoming highly influential and making a huge impact throughout the world.

(February) The Web is the main reason for the theme of the G7 meeting hosted by the European Commission in the European Parliament buildings in Brussels.

(March) CERN holds a two-day seminar for the European Media (press, radio, TV), attended by 250 reporters, to show www. It is demonstrated on 60 machines, with 30 pupils from the local International High School helping the reporters "surf the Web".

(April) The Third International www Conference: "Tools and Applications", is hosted by the Fraunhofer Gesellschaft in Darmstadt (DE).

(June) We see the founding of the Web Society in Graz (AT), by the Technical University of Graz (home of Hyper-G), CERN, the University of Minnesota (home of Gopher) and INRIA.

Yusuf is now in the Philippines. Here, local intelligence agencies working with the CIA arrest Abdul Muraili with a laptop in a bomb kitchen. But Yusuf manages to escape to Singapore

1998

From here onwards the usage and development of the www proceeds at a rapid pace enabled by the ready availability of personal computers and of more sophisticated browser systems. This process continues to develop.

(May) Osama Bin Laden declares war on the USA.

(7th August) Al Qaeda bomb the USA Embassy in Kenya and bomb other premises in Tanzania.

2001

(11th September) Al Qaeda operatives hijack four civil aircraft. They fly two into the twin towers of the World Trade Center in New York; one into the Pentagon; and the fourth which is thought to be aiming to destroy the White House crashes after passengers bravely intervene. Thousands of people die in the four

Continued overleaf

A Short History of the World Wide Web	A Short History of Al Qaeda
	aircraft crashes in what is undoubtedly the worse terrorist incident ever known.
2002	(12th October) '9/11' is followed by bombings by Al Qaeda operatives in night clubs in Bali, which appear to be aimed at Western tourists, indiscriminately killing and maiming innocent travellers.
2004	(September) Al Qaeda operatives strike in Spain, placing bombs on several crowded commuter trains, indiscriminately killing and maiming innocent travellers.
2005	(July) Muslim bombers strike in London where four suicide bombers explode bombs on the London Underground and on a bus during the busy rush hour, indiscriminately killing and maiming many innocent travellers.
	(July) Al Qaeda operatives strike in Egypt using truck bombs to blow up hotels and aimed at Western tourists, indiscriminately killing and maiming many innocent local workers and travellers.
	(October) A further attack by Al Qaeda operatives on a restaurant in Bali also appears to be aimed at Western tourists, indiscriminately killing and maiming many innocent local workers and travellers.
	In all of these terrorist attacks there has been a heavy loss of life and massive damage. Al Qaeda claim responsibility for each of these attacks and those sought or arrested are known members of Al Qaeda, or at the very least have been inspired by Al Qaeda.

Directly or indirectly, www is now part of the everyday life of nearly everyone. By providing quick and easy access to a multitude of information, it has opened up enormous possibilities throughout the world. What seems so surprising when presented in this way is the relatively short life span of www. What seems to have been part of our life for ages has really only been available to us for a short period. As is shown in the above table it was in 1993 that the real breakthrough was made when CERN made their knowledge available free to anyone and it then became available on PC Windows and Mackintosh systems making www available to virtually anyone with a personal computer. By 1995 it was seen to be having a huge impact on members of societies throughout the world. Thus we might trace back to 1995 and onwards as the moment that Globalization was seen to be having such a disruptive effect on societies throughout the world: the moment when societal culture became more of a "dynamic process" than being "evidenced by sameness and continuity". This in itself tends to support the argument that Globalization has had a huge impact on societies throughout the world. That is a matter that will be the subject of a much fuller and deeper discussion in later chapters.

At the same time we will be aware that by any measure the activities of Osama Bin Laden and his Al Qaeda followers have been without precedent. The scale and nature of the terrorist activities carried out by Bin Laden and others in the name of Al Qaeda has been at a level only previously experienced in wartime. As with the development of the www, so the development of Al Qaeda has been a relatively recent phenomenon. Viewing the development of terrorism in this way enables us to see the way that it has built and escalated in recent years in much the same way as the www. We can also see how Osama Bin Laden became known to the world at about the same time as the development of www, and how his rise, and that of Al Qaeda, coincides with the rise of Globalization. The 1993 attack on the World Trade Center coincided with the date that www was made available to all; and the 9/11 plot was in being in 1995 when Globalization was being driven by the www.

Having shown the uncanny way that the undoubted driver of Globalization, the www, and the main global Muslim terrorist response, Al Qaeda, have developed in parallel we may agree that there is something compelling about the notion that there is a mutuality and connectedness between the two. However, this is but a skeleton and to flesh out the body of the argument requires that we need to go much deeper. In particular we need to understand the inter-cultural conflict that has developed as one of the consequences of Globalization. I'm going to start that deeper process of exploration by referring to the experience of history. In particular that period of history that is now being called the "first Globalization": the Industrial Revolution that is generally accepted to have covered a total period of 59 years from 1789–1848.

CHAPTER THREE

The Industrial Revolution: the first Globalization

T his chapter, in reviewing and reflecting on selective aspects of the historical period known as the Industrial Revolution, seeks to provide a further context for today's Globalization. The experiences of nearly two hundred years ago will not replicate the unique experiences of today but they provide us with some very powerful indicators of what to expect from such revolutionary activities. There are so many important and interesting similarities in the dynamics that arose as a consequence of the Industrial Revolution and those that are currently arising as a consequence of Globalization, that it would be foolish to ignore them. Such are the similarities that this period has now become known as the first Globalization; or Globalization One. The changes at the time of the Industrial Revolution were doubtless as imperceptible then as they are now. But with the aid of hindsight we can see that then, as now, the depth and breadth of the changes were such that it must have been experienced as "death of a way of life", and the problems of adjusting to a new way of life must have been as stressful as they are today.

There are many important aspects of the Industrial Revolution but one of the most important matters arising from knowing and appreciating something of this period is that it provides us with an important reminder of past Western activities. No period of history has left a richer legacy in the popular imagination and this stays on in the world of today. It was not only a period of great industrial and economic change and achievement but it was also the period of Wellington and the defeat of Napoleon at Waterloo and of Nelson and his great victory at Trafalgar. From this period we really do carry our own history about with us, which is important in terms of relatedness. The way that we in Britain and the West and that others in societies throughout the world carry the history of the time with us today continues to have a mutual effect on both Western and non-Western societies.

Much of the history that we carry with us today concerns those activities that will have had a lasting impact on non-Western cultures. The sort of matters which those members of other societies and cultures will have cause to remember; and which we in the West have cause to forget. It will also show how some of the same activities are being repeated, as are the consequences. The Industrial Revolution had a major impact on the whole way of life that affected societies throughout the world. A current difficulty, and one experienced by those who lived through the period of the Industrial Revolution, is that other than having a general sense that something revolutionary was happening it is exceedingly difficult to be able to have a clear understanding at this time. One of the aims of this chapter is to use the experience of the Industrial Revolution to show how members of societies throughout the world responded in trying to cope with the consequences of developing a new way of life. I will particularly show the way that members of society responded by becoming extremely dependent, turning to religion and seeking a Messianic figure to lead them out of their despair; and how they sometimes responded by rebellion and violent actions against the authorities of the time.

Specific areas covered will be the effect of the first Globalization on Western societies and culture; the effect on non-Western societies and culture; and the effect on religion. Where appropriate, attention will be drawn to current-day experiences where they are seen to be similar to those of the first Globalization. However, I want to start the exploration by referring to the way the first Globalization began. As we shall see in the following chapter, Globalization started from a position of economic failure, as also did the Industrial Revolution.

As is currently happening, out of that position of relative failure the Industrial Revolution transformed the entire world. It took the form of a European expansion in and conquest of the rest of the world. Indeed its most striking consequence was to establish a domination of the globe by a few Western regimes, and especially by the British. But as we shall see, this was not to the advantage of all concerned, whether that be in Europe or the rest of the world, as will be further discussed later in the chapter. For now though I shall return to the circumstances out of which the Industrial Revolution developed.

International rivalry, especially war, tests the resources of a state as nothing else does. When nations overspend they quickly begin to crumble and fall, and in a sense this is the beginning of the Industrial Revolution. One major rivalry, the conflict between Britain and France, dominated the European international scene for most of the eighteenth century, and lay at the core of its recurrent periods of general war. By any reckoning, France was the most powerful, eminent and influential nation; it was the classical, aristocratic, absolute monarchy but competition and rivalry led to its downfall. After being defeated by Britain in the Seven Years War (1756–63), the revolt of the American colonies against British rule gave France the opportunity to turn the tables on its adversary by going to the aid of the Americans in the subsequent War of Independence between 1778 and 1783. Britain was badly defeated, losing the most important part of her American empire. However, in going to the aid of the American colonists the French ruined their finances and were in so much difficulty that it ultimately and near inevitably led France into that period of domestic political crisis, out of which six years later the French Revolution emerged. The effect on Britain was barely felt and they were soon to be taking the opportunity for trading with the new United States of America. Meanwhile, Britain was in the process of their own revolution, one which was achieved not by any great external event, nor by any sudden insurrection of the people, but by the creativity and skill of the people—not to mention a vast source of cheap labour. That is not to ignore the fact that the changes did shake the foundations, as will be seen below.

There was so much change, most of it unprecedented, during the second half of the eighteenth century that this period in human history has been regarded as the great divide between past and present. It is said to have been the true beginning of modern times.

The period of the Industrial Revolution was such that no parallels could be found in history, and for the first time the past ceased to throw its light upon the future. The period was one of formative changes in the structure of the English economy, the shape of English society, and the framework of government. On the one hand was the new economic power unleashed by the development of a coal and iron technology; on the other, the problems posed by its use. To those who lived through this period the discoveries and developments of their generation seemed to bring a level of achievement to Britain that would not be attainable through conquest or dominion. Agricultural and mechanical improvements had produced changes unparalleled in the chronicles of the world. Porter in *The Progress of Nations* (1847) said that, "in his own lifetime he had seen the greatest advances in civilization that can be found recorded in the annals of mankind".

As with Globalization there is nothing as simple as an available definition of the Industrial Revolution. It meant different things to different people and was an all-encompassing economic, social and political revolution. However, we can say that the following characteristics of the time were: a new relationship between man and nature, expressed in the exploitation of physical power and the use of machinery; the rise of a new class structure, conceived of, usually explicitly, in "class" terms, and dependent on a massive working-class base; a transformation of politics and administration, so that the control of oligarchies was diminished and the influence of "opinion" was given greater play; an improvement of manners and morals among both "high" and "low"; and the determination of new attitudes and policies in international relations.

The rise of British power in the world and the creation of an "intellectual empire" as well as a "workshop of all the nations" seemed to be related to each other, each feature being a part of the same complex of progress. A measure of the profundity of change is that throughout Britain, the spread of industrialization changed forever the notion of time. The lives of the workers, who included children, were now regulated by the factory hooter. Work started early and went on late. There were battles between workers and employers about hours as well as wages. Faster coaches pulled by horses introduced "timetables" before the age of the steam locomotive and the use of standard railway time. Foreigners often complained of the

English mania for "saving time". Yet, as we will now be well aware, speed was to attract people in most countries, whatever their history. A further example is the way that throughout the world during this period the British expansionist process continued unabated and distant frontiers of adventure and exploitation drew English men and English money from the confines of this small island. The expansion was not confined to the formal Empire but to the contact of English and foreign cultures anywhere in the world.

With hindsight we can see that which was hidden from the view of those who were alive at the time and this allows us to make an assessment of what to them was their immediate past. As today, the generations alive during this period were generally aware that their economy and society had undergone a profound transformation within living memory. But it is clear that they had little to add to this level of awareness. In living through this period of transaction from one way of life to another it was simply not possible to predict the future or to understand the current position at any given time. With the help of hindsight, however, we can now see what those living at that time were unable to see and this provides us with a valuable window on the dynamics of today. In a general sense even with the benefit of hindsight the word "revolution" is still as highly appropriate as it is today. And as a general guide to when we might make sense of the current revolution, we might bear in mind that it was not until the 1860s that people could begin to see the whole process of the Industrial Revolution in perspective. Even with the help of hindsight it is clear that the pace of change was not perceived as anything but rapid and astonishing.

The fact that the Industrial Revolution was initiated by Britain was not fortuitous. As explained above, having seen off the main competition (France), Britain was left with a relatively free hand to develop their creative talents on a worldwide stage. Nowhere is the superiority of the new to the old social order more vividly exemplified than in the conflict between these powers. For the British not only won, with varying degrees of decisiveness in all but one of the wars in which they were engaged, but most importantly they supported the effort of organizing, financing and waging wars with relative ease. The basic reason was that even before the Industrial Revolution, Britain was far ahead of the French in per capita output and trade. By then more than a century had passed since King

Charles I had been formally tried and executed by the British people, and since then private profit and economic development had become accepted as the guiding principles of government policy. Unlike France, which was wedded to an absolute Monarchy that required to be supported by a huge funding supplied by the people, Britain had a constitutional Monarchy and the right conditions for growth were visibly present in Britain.

The name Industrial Revolution reflects its relatively tardy impact on Europe. The process existed long before the word. As was mentioned in the Preface, Globalization does not generally attract very much publicity. It is truly imperceptible to most members of societies, at least at a fully conscious level, and that seems to be the case in the first Globalization. It was not until the 1820s that English and French socialists—themselves a newly created group—invented the term "Industrial Revolution", probably by analogy with the political revolution of France. This is very similar to the experience of Globalization. As was shown in Chapter Two, the only meaningful way of establishing a date when Globalization could be seen to have begun was by relating to the history of the www. Until recently Globalization has had an equally tardy impact on the world. Members of societies today, as was the case with those in the Industrial Revolution, know that our economies and societies are undergoing a profound transformation but it seems nigh impossible to go past these generalizations. The current Globalization has been compared with and referred to as a revolution that I feel is highly appropriate. However, it would appear that the word "revolution" is "off message" and Globalization is a more acceptable word in this age.

That words are important, as referred to by E. J. Hobsbawn in *The Age of Revolution* (1962), where he reminds us that words are witnesses which often speak louder than documents. And he invites us to consider a few English words that were invented, or gained their modern meanings, substantially in the period of 60 years between 1789 and 1848. They are such words as "industry", "industrialist", "factory", "middle class", "working class", "capitalist" and "socialism". They include "aristocracy" as well as "railway", "liberal" and "conservative" as political terms, "nationality", "scientist" and "engineer", "proletariat" and "economic" (crisis), "utilitarian" and "statistics", "sociology" and several other names of modern sciences, "journalism" and "ideology", all coinages or adaptations of this period. So is "strike" and "pauperism".

To imagine the modern world without these words, that is, without the things and concepts for which they provide names, is to measure the profundity of the revolution that broke out in this period. Only in retrospect can we understand the true effects of the changes in the way of life of ordinary people in both Western and non-Western societies. For many in Britain, the only life they had ever known was one of working on the land as subsistence farmers. They were working to survive and depending on the success of their work lived well or not so well. What, then, must have been the effect of this huge upheaval and movement of thousands of people to the towns and cities? From a life of relative freedom of choice to one of being controlled in the new factories must in all likelihood, as now, been experienced as "death of a way of life".

The words developed at the time of the Industrial Revolution are now so much part of our taken-for-granted assumptions that it is difficult to realise that society was once so very different. In testimony to Hobsbawn's thesis that words are witnesses that often speak louder than documents I invite you to consider some of the English words that have been invented, or gained their modern meanings, in the last decade or so. Words such as "internet", "information super highway", "worldwide web", "virtual reality", "CD-ROM", "fibre optics", "digital highway", "computer-integrated manufacturing (CIM)", "micro-chip", "Globalization", and many others too numerous to mention. These words are also witnesses that speak louder than documents. And, these words have become part of our taken-for-granted assumptions in a rapidly changing world. One of the most significant facts about these words and especially the "others" not mentioned, is that there will be many members of society who do not fully or even totally understand them. This I consider to be an indication and support for the notion that we are still far from the end of Globalization.

It is as well to consider the name "Industrial Revolution" for two reasons. First because it "broke out" before the Bastille was stormed and second because without it we cannot understand the impersonal groundswell of history on which the more obvious men and events of the period were borne; the uneven complexity of its rhythm. In Chapter Two, I tried to show how Globalization developed over a period starting in or even before 1985; but that it did not "break out" until about 1995. As was the Industrial Revolution before it, Globalization is a dynamic process that is constantly changing and in a state of flux, and as such it is exceedingly difficult to pin it down to specific dates. The dynamic history of Globalization is perhaps evidenced by the lack of media references to Globalization referred to in the Preface. In addition, I feel sure that the term "Globalization" has not always been well defined, intentionally or because of its developmental nature, with a result that it has meant many things to many people. I believe that something of its true meaning is only currently becoming known.

What does the phrase "the Industrial Revolution broke out" mean? It means that some time in the 1780s, and for the first time in human history, the shackles were taken off the productive power of human societies, which henceforth became capable of the constant, rapid and up to the present limitless multiplication of men, goods and services. This is technically known to the economists now as the "take off into sustained growth". The Industrial Revolution was not an episode with a beginning and an end. It is senseless to ask when it was "complete", for its essence was that henceforth revolutionary change became the norm. We might equally ask what would the phrase "Globalization broke out" mean? As we shall see later in this chapter the new technologies of the Industrial Revolution created a continuing transformation over a long period. Who at that time could say where it was going to take them? Seeing Globalization from the above perspective of the Industrial Revolution enables us to understand that it is bound to be difficult to identify the start position of Globalization and while we may not be able to answer this question with any more certainty than our forefathers, we can gain a deeper understanding from the experiences they had at the time of the Industrial Revolution. It also helps us to understand that there will be no point when we say that this is the end.

It may be useful to consider what it was about that period that led it to be regarded as revolutionary. Clearly, it was not just the change in technology, but the fact that the new technology brought into being a new way of living. The creativity of the Industrial Revolution was really a triumph not so much of industry but of capitalist industry, it transformed and continues to transform the entire world. It took the form of a European expansion in and conquest of the rest of the world. Indeed its most striking consequence was to establish a domination of the globe by a few Western regimes, especially the British. It was led by, and powered by, the merchants, the steam engines, the ships and the guns of the West. But equally importantly by its ideas – including political, philosophic and religious ideas. Faced with such an all-encompassing and powerful assault on their way of life, the age-old civilizations and empires of the world capitulated and collapsed. Clearly, this was not just an Industrial Revolution. It was simply not possible to invade other countries and take their resources. The required human resources were also vital to Western success. The process had to be supported by the military, bureaucratic and administrative procedures.

In short, it was far from being solely an Industrial Revolution but was also a political and social revolution. The more like "us" that we could make "them" in other societies the more successful would be the process. Hence, there was a desire to change that most significant of differences—the religions. In the Industrial Revolution the missionaries backed by the military "invaded" other societies and attempted to thrust Western religion on them, whether they wanted it or not. Whether this was a deliberate or unconscious intent, it seems that the purpose was to convert them from the values of the barbaric to those of Western society. It was a cynical and monocular view of Western supremacy. Today we see a similar process which is probably part deliberate and part unconscious; I refer to the way that democracy is thrust forward with near missionary zeal as a model of goodness and virtue, whether those concerned want it or not. In the case of Iraq it is much the same as occurred in the Industrial Revolution when missionaries were backed by the military.

Global expansion meant that India became a province administered by Britain; the Islamic states were convulsed by crisis; Africa lay open to direct conquest; and, even the Chinese Empire in the period 1839–1842 was forced to open its doors to Western exploitation. This first Globalization allowed Britain and others to take full advantage of the breakthroughs in technological and theoretical creativity and the effect was that the Industrial Revolution meant that European countries were able to apply their political, legal, social and economic methods to the entire world. Compared with today, this all seems very familiar with many of the same world players involved. Capitalist industries in the shape of multi-national conglomerates are the vehicles that are leading the Globalization effort. Is the aim the same? Or perhaps a more pertinent question might be is the aim perceived as the same? Is it perceived as an attempt by the USA and other Western countries to dominate the Globe? These are important questions that I shall return to in later chapters. But I first want to consider some of the effects of the Industrial Revolution on British and other Western societies.

British social conditions

It will perhaps help to get some sort of picture of the conditions under which people were living in Britain at this time and their response to this "new way of life". In 1780 eighty percent of British people were living in the countryside. Outside London, large towns like Birmingham, Bristol, and Liverpool each consisted of about 50,000 inhabitants. By 1830 great manufacturing towns had sprung up in Manchester (182,000 population), Leeds (123,000), Birmingham (144,000), and Liverpool (202,000). In this relatively short space of time, the links with the countryside were broken forever and the rural village community was replaced with something else. One culture replaced another and to all appearances this was irreversibly so. Not the least of the reasons for irreversibility is that the new organization could support a much larger population than the old. Once the population had increased to the extent that the change permitted, a return to the earlier conditions was impossible.

Deprived of the traditional institutions and guides to behaviour that were present in country living, a result was that many could not but fail to sink into an abyss of hand to mouth expedients. There is every reason to believe that the experience for large numbers of British and European societies was a threat to or loss of identity. The subsequent feelings of chaos and hopelessness had to be coped with in some way. A measure of the psychological disturbance at the time is the way that vast numbers of society sought escape through the use of alcohol. Mass alcoholism was an almost invariable companion of headlong and uncontrolled industrialization and urbanization spread and there was "a pestilence of hard liquor" across

Europe. There was also an upsurge of temperance organizations, but these sought to treat the symptoms and not the causes. To be fair to those concerned it is doubtful if anything could stop the causes. Progress towards a new way of life arising from the process of the first Globalization was all-encompassing and continuing at a rapid pace.

Rebellion

There were increasing and mounting debates on three interrelated basic social questions: the size of the population; the state of the poor; and the provision of education. The question of the poor was eventually settled when they abolished all outside relief for the poor and forced them into "workhouses". It was believed that individuals would become more self-reliant, public money would be saved and the care of the poor, previously associated with charity, would be systematized. Conditions for the inmates of workhouses were to be made deliberately worse than those on the worst forms of alternative employment so as to avoid large-scale economic dependency. However, in the longer run opposition to the Poor Law of 1834, which set up the workhouse system, played a major part in triggering off the great protest movement of Chartism, the first specifically large-scale working class movement in Europe. In spite of the remarkable advances and resultant wealth created by the new economic power the problems resulting from its use presented social dynamics that required equally creative responses. Part of this was the notion of organized labour and in industrializing Britain the words "labour movement" were used as early as 1828. However, rebellion was seemingly ever-present beneath the surface and was never far from breaking out into violent protest.

With the benefit of hindsight it is clear that politicians never took stability for granted. They were continually aware of small groups committed to revolution and they knew that such groups succeeded at various times in producing embryonic revolutionary organizations and plotting violent political activities. They also knew at this time that society harboured a much larger reservoir of less focused political frustrations and radical aspirations. Successive governments feared revolutionary violence, and as apparent need appeared, the authorities used military force, political surveillance and legal repression to contain it. The Luddite's, a name that has since become synonymous with those rejecting change, were a group of activists who engaged in machine wrecking as a revolt against unemployment resulting from the introduction of machinery. These activities and those of the Chartist movement and others produced a flood of extremist pamphlets, placards and newspapers advocating the overthrow of the state. They also produced genuine revolutionary conspiracies. For example, we may presume that the Cato Street conspirators, so named after a group that met at that location, and who were engaged in an unsuccessful plot to kill the person responsible for a Massacre of protesters at a place called Peterloo, actually intended to assassinate the British Cabinet in 1820, and that their plot, however ineffective, was merely one dangerous eddy amid others in the political turbulence of a volatile society.

New machinery was one of the chief benefits to be expected from private enterprise and free competition. But there was a resistance from even the "ruling class" to such aspects of pure individual free competition that did not actually benefit them personally. On the other hand many if not most were totally committed to the artificial protection for their businesses. But it was not only the labouring Luddites that arose to smash the machinery. In some instances the smaller businessmen and farmers in their regions sympathized with them because they also regarded innovators as destroyers of men's livelihood. Farmers actually left their machinery out for rioters to destroy. We can be sure that the societal culture was also playing its part in resisting the changes in the way of life. Seen from a society-as-a-whole perspective we can view the Luddites as doing something on behalf of society. Seeing the new machinery as the symbolic representation of change the Luddites were mobilized to destroy it on behalf of society.

Although professing their support for free trade, during the Industrial Revolution the British used protectionism. The free traders were against both the newly formed Trade Unions and legislation regulating working conditions. They were for high wages and well run factories, providing the owners made those decisions. Dissatisfied workers were told that if they didn't like it they should emigrate. The pro-democracy group, the Chartists, wanted precisely the same democratic rules that Western democracies have today. However, this did not meet with the wishes of the mill owners and the free traders were not supportive. The Chartists were gradually marginalized, which pushed them into violence with a result that many were arrested, tried and deported.

We should not underestimate the inhumanity and injustice that accompanied the early stages of the Industrial Revolution. At the time, this was met by political and social leaders with a sort of social blindness. But of course the contemporaries who deplored the demoralization of the new urban and industrialized poor were not exaggerating. Everything, the whole experience, combined to maximize it. As described above, towns and industrial areas grew rapidly, without plan or supervision, and the most elementary services of city life utterly failed to keep pace with the level of growth. Street cleaning, water supply, sanitation, not to mention working-class housing, were all inadequate. But the most obvious consequence was disease, notably cholera, which took its toll on many of the new working class and their families.

There are similarities with what is happening in Western societies today. Immigrant labour, much of it illegal, is employed to perform the physical societal tasks that members of the indigenous community will not perform. Deliberately being outside the formal systems, they are paid a relative pittance and enjoy no rights and privileges. They live in crowded and poor living conditions where again they cannot demand the usual rights provided by the laws of the land. Recently in America a million people took to the streets to demonstrate in favour of the immigrants. In other countries it has resulted in other forms of action every bit as violent as that of the rebellious groups who were mobilized during the Industrial Revolution. In non-Western societies the cheap labour is exploited to provide cheap goods for Western consumption. In these other countries there are thousands of people who have migrated from the villages of rural areas to the cities to seek work. Here they experience poor working conditions, long hours, and poor living conditions: in other words, the same sort of experience as that of the British people in the Industrial Revolution.

As painful as the situation must have been there was no real means of escape and the only real alternative was rebellion. And such was the situation of the labouring poor that rebellion was not merely possible but virtually compulsory. The appearance of organized labour and socialist movements, and of mass social revolutionary unrest, was the main vehicle for rebellion. The concept and the word "socialism" was created in the 1820s and this was soon to result in the creation of the mass movement previously referred to and known as the Chartists. A measure of the rebellious mood of the working class was talk of a general strike by Chartists. And a more serious attempt by the Chartists to use a purely trade unionist model not only to fight for higher wages but to attempt to defeat the entire existing society and establish a new one was made in 1829 and 1834. Where campaigns aimed too high or were perceived as too frightening by the ruling class they failed. A measure of the climate that this organized resistance was creating is that in the hysterical 1810s the tendency was to call out the armed forces against any serious demonstration.

Mainly as a result of unemployment and bad harvests, in 1817 radical meetings were organized in cities throughout the country. Members of the government responded by trying to pass Acts seeking to suppress freedom of the press and free assembly. The result was several bloody occurrences that passed into the history of the organized labour movement. Some of the bloodiest and most notable were the Peterloo Massacre in Manchester in 1819 when an open air meeting in support of parliamentary reform was charged by yeomanry killing eleven people and wounding a further five hundred. A further significant event concerned a group of six farm labourers who in 1834, at a place called Tolpuddle in the south of England, were transported to Australia for forming a trade union. This group became known as the Tolpuddle Martyrs and after nationwide agitation they were pardoned two years later.

The use of the military, the severe sentences, and the formal legal attempts to suppress freedom of the press, and freedom of assembly, demonstrate the extreme experiences of members of British society at this time. There can be little doubt that then, as now, they must have been experiencing death of a way of life and all the feelings of loss of identity and fragmentation that went with it. It also shows us something of the reactions of those in authority when faced with uncertainty and an inability to foresee the immediate future. It is interesting to compare these actions with those of today's authorities. In Britain there have been many Acts passed that have the effect of suppressing freedoms that members of society have long accepted as unchallengeable. In America, executive decisions have been made regarding the interception of communications. And extreme measures such as the facilities used at Guantanamo Bay have been set up to avoid the rights of prisoners normally accorded by American law.

Colonization

There is a further interesting contemporary parallel here with the question of working conditions in factories in developing countries where goods are being produced by cheap labour. Today those workers play exactly the same sort of role played by the Western working class in the nineteenth century. Then as now the standard argument was that any attempt to regulate the workplace would damage the market and hurt the workers. Employment was their opportunity to better themselves and if they didn't like it they would move the factories elsewhere. If do-gooders were allowed to interfere, the market would go elsewhere. Thus it is in this Globalization that we have seen the market move from one country to another in an attempt to maintain low costs of production.

We might reasonably assume that if this was the way that members of British society were treated, then those in other societies, in other lands, might expect to be treated at least the same. Guided by the social aspect of the revolution, where the European middle class came into contact with the unbelieving heathens, they sought to convert them through intellectually unsophisticated missionaries to the truths of Christianity, commerce, and rather unbelievingly the wearing of trousers or imposing on them the truths of liberal legislation. If, as the French suggested, they accepted these conditions, they would be perfectly prepared to grant them full citizenship with all its rights. This attitude is perfectly represented in an edict by Napoleon III which stated that for Algerians to become equal, they could be so, all they had to give up, in effect, was Islam. If they did not want to do so—and few did—then they remained a subject and not a citizen. Or as the British put it: the hope of one day being almost as good as an Englishman. I have little doubt that these are matters they we would rather forget. Equally, we may be sure that these are matters that have not been forgotten by those who were subjected to this treatment.

During this period, the massive contempt of the "civilized" for the stereotypical "barbarians", and this included the bulk of the labouring poor at home, rested on a feeling of demonstrated superiority. In essence, the middle class world was freely open to all, but few were able to pass the stringent tests permitting entry. The effect was that those who failed to enter its gates were therefore seen as demonstrating a lack of personal intelligence, moral force or energy which automatically condemned them; or at best, they were attributed to an historic or racial heritage which must permanently cripple them. If not it was assumed that they would already have made use of their opportunities. They were stereotyped not as second-class citizens but as non-citizens and treated that way. The emotional learning from that time is to be found in traces of this historic legacy in industrial disputes to this day. Internationally, the Industrial Revolution resulted in colonization of many countries for a century or more. With the emotional learning from these experiences, might they reasonably fear that Globalization is a further attempt at colonization?

Religion

For most members of societies anywhere, religion is part of our internalized values and beliefs, not to mention our conscience. Each of us develops our own set of values. By means of the primitive process of introjection we take in values which then form internal mental images which become part of our stock of knowledge. An attitude represents the interplay of a person's emotions, cognitions, and behavioural tendencies with regard to something—another person or group, an event, an idea and so on—in the individual's organizational or social world. Beliefs and attitudes often combine to form all-encompassing ideals called values. A value is established when a belief or concept is enduring and provides a personally preferable mode of conduct. Often a value is the sum total of many attitudes that when taken together provide personal commitment and consistency, for example "honesty" and "fairness" are values, as is religious belief. For members of societies to change their values and attitudes, whatever they may be, indicates that something immensely powerful is occurring.

Of the many consequences arising from the Industrial Revolution, the effect on religion is vital to our understanding of today. During this period, as now, there was a considerable increase in religious activity and a considerable change in the sort of religions that were being followed. I believe this is symptomatic of the degree of upheaval in societies arising out of the effects of the Industrial Revolution. When traditional societies change something as fundamental as their religion, it is clear that they must be facing major new problems. Precisely how the people of Africa and Asia experienced the effects of the Industrial Revolution we cannot say with any certainty but "major new problems" seems hopelessly naïve compared with what must have been a huge emotional shock. It seems more likely that they must really have felt that they were experiencing "death of a way of life". In many societies the defensive process that we know as "identification with the aggressor" doubtless resulted in many members of non-Western societies throughout the world bowing to the general and specific pressure of missionaries to become Christians, so that they would become like the aggressors.

Two types of religion showed a particular aptitude for expansion in the period of the Industrial Revolution: Islam and evangelical Protestantism. When we consider the rise in population associated with this period we might well expect that the interest in religious activity was likely to expand. And expand it did, but this expansionism was in the non-Established churches and Islam. This contrasted with the marked failure of other Christian religions—both Catholic and Protestant—to expand. This was even more surprising because it occurred, in spite of the sharp increase in missionary activity, outside Europe, which was increasingly backed by the military, political and economic force of European penetration. There was a whole host of Protestant missionary activity which for example included, in the 1820s, the Swedish Society, and representatives of churches in nearly all European countries. It may be an indication of the power of the churches and religion that missionary activity was so high on the agenda for change.

If we accept the notion that "there must be major problems when society changes something as fundamental as its religion" we need also to accept that there must have been major problems at home. The expansionist movement of evangelical Protestant religion differs from that of Islam in that it was almost entirely confined to the countries of developed capitalist civilization. Its extent cannot be measured, for some movements of this kind remained within the framework of their respective established state churches. However, its size is not in doubt. In 1851 roughly half the Protestant worshippers in England and Wales attended religious services other than those of the Established Church. This extraordinary triumph of the evangelical churches was the result, in the main, of religious developments since 1790, or more precisely since the last years of the Napoleonic Wars. Thus, in 1790 the Wesleyan Methodists had only 59,000 communicant members in the UK; in 1850 they and their various offshoots had ten times that number.

By the 1790s Methodism was the most conspicuous and successful manifestation of a spectacular social and religious movement that had swept large areas of the country creating unconventional forms of association, social behaviour and thought among artisans, trades people, small freeholders, labourers and a sprinkling of professional people. This new popular evangelicalism, by challenging the spiritual and ecclesiastical authority of the Church of England, had already achieved considerable social significance by the end of the eighteenth century. This was perhaps inevitable in a society with an Established Church. For a church by law established, is by virtue of its establishment a social and political institution, not just a narrowly religious one, and it was at that time literally part of the state. Its aim was seen as complementing the work of the civil power.

Methodism was different to the other dissenting traditions of the Presbyterians, Congregationalists, Baptists and Quakers. It began as a conversionist evangelical movement within the Church of England but conflict soon developed between the Established Church and the Methodists. A result was that countless Methodists suffered injury, indignity and loss at the hands of anti-Methodist mobs. It was evidence of a widespread belief that the new movement was a form of social as well as religious deviance. Those who became Methodists were the kinds of people who, in matters of politics, industrial relations or social status, often found themselves at odds, in one way or another, with the norms, values, and institutions of the ruling classes. There would appear to be good grounds for concluding that religious deviance such as that provided by the Methodists was a political "safety valve" for the pressures of early industrial politics.

In other societies where the general and specific pressure of missionaries was either not present or was ineffective, waiting to fill the void were the Moslem traders, who had a virtual monopoly of the commerce of inner Africa with the outside world and multiplied with it, helping to bring Islam to the notice of new peoples. The slave trade which broke down communal life made it attractive, for Islam is a powerful means of reintegrating social structures. At the same time the Islamic religion appealed to the semi-feudal and military societies of the Sudan, and its sense of independence, militancy and superiority made it a useful counterweight to slavery. As against the aggressive approach of Western religions, Islam was continuing that silent, piecemeal and irreversible expansion unsupported by organized missionary endeavour or forcible conversion, which is so characteristic of that religion. It expanded both eastwards in Indonesia and North-western China, and westwards from the Sudan towards Senegal and, to a much smaller extent, from the shores of the Indian Ocean inland. During this period, the map of Islam was drawn ever wider and at the end of the period resembled what it is today. The ferment and expansion of Islam was such that in terms of purely religious history, we can perhaps best describe the period from 1789 to 1848 as that of a world of Islamic revival. It would appear that history is repeating itself today. Faced again with threats to their individual and group identity people in Western and non-Western societies have sought some sort of saviour. In many non-Western societies they have turned to Islam.

Then as now, Islam was openly resistant to Western colonization. While the element of resistance to the whites was clearly very small in the sparse influence of African Islam, it was by tradition crucial in South-east Asia. Unlike those who supported other religions, which in the main would have been animistic religions, Islam did not weaken. It had long advanced against local cults and the declining Hinduism of the spice islands largely as a means of more effective resistance against the Portuguese and Dutch, as a kind of "pre-nationalism", though also as a popular counterweight to the Hinduized princes. Even in those days, Islam was not prepared to compromise.

As was the case within the Christian religions where the evangelical churches came into conflict with the Established church so also were there challenges within the Islamic faith. Within Islam the movements of reform and revival, which in this period gave the religion much of its penetrative power, can also be seen as reflecting the impact of European expansion and the crisis of the old Mohammedan societies, notably of the Turkish and Persian empires. In the period 1814–1840 more puritanical versions of Islam inspired by strong willed individual leaders developed in Arabia, Syria, Egypt, Algeria, Persia, Afghanistan, and India. This seems to mirror the way that strong willed individual Islamic leaders are currently opposing Western values and policies. It may be a strong indicator that the experience of non-Western societies at the time of the Industrial Revolution was very similar to that of today. We see the results of these developments today in the various branches of Islam such as, but not solely, the Shiites and the Sunnis. We also see a contemporary conflict between Muslim nations largely based on the brand of Islamic religion that they support.

The effect on religion was so widespread that we must assume that many nations were affected by the Industrial Revolution. As we shall see when we refer to Globalization this is precisely the case today. There was no equivalent mass movement developed in any other non-Christian religion. Although, near the end of the period of the Industrial Revolution the great Chinese Taiping rebellion, which has many characteristics of a mass movement, was beginning to create a growing crisis in the Chinese Empire. That there should be rebellion in China is perhaps not surprising given some of the effects of the Industrial Revolution. Critical among these was the activity of the British, who, in 1781, wanting trade with China but having no ready means of finance came up with a novel idea. Having no money to pay for goods they insisted on paying the Chinese with Indian Opium for the required British imports. The effect on the Chinese population is well known and something that we would wish to forget, but it is unlikely that they have forgotten. A measure of the British approach to this immoral trade is that attempts by the British Parliament to abolish the practice were defeated in 1870, 1875, 1886 and 1889. It was not until 1913 that it was finally ceased.

In the United States a very similar process of mass conversion multiplied the number of Baptists, Methodists and to a lesser extent

Presbyterians at the relative expense of the formerly dominant churches; by 1850 almost three-quarters of all churches in the USA belonged to these three denominations. The disruption of established churches, the secession and rise of sects, also marks the religious history of this period in Scotland, the Netherlands, Norway and other countries. Why, we might ask, did members of Western societies desert the Established churches? I would hypothesise that the established churches were seen as part of the existing institutions that had failed to provide containment and support at a time when the experience was one of hopelessness, disorientation and a loss of or threat to their identity. In these circumstances they sought an alternative saviour in the shape of the non-established churches. As will be seen in the next chapter history appears to be repeating itself through the massive increase in evangelical religion in the United States.

By 1848 expansion turned into contraction. At this stage, in the Islamic world we can begin to observe the first stages of a revolt against the West, that process by which those conquered by the West have adopted its ideas and techniques to turn the tables on it. This is an important aspect of the Industrial Revolution and one that may be even more significant and have greater implications for Globalization. In 1848, communication and learning was slow and limited. Today, in the computerized world of the www communication, learning and access to information is incredibly fast and comprehensive. In effect there is no reason why other countries should not be leading out their own form of Globalization. By the end of 1848 the spectre of communism already haunted Europe. This historic period begins with the construction of the first factory in Lancashire, England; ends with the construction of its first railway network; and the publication of the Communist Manifesto.

By 1867 foresighted contemporaries were increasingly uncertain about the future. They could anticipate continued speed of change in years to come, but they were less sure about direction. In 1864 Froude wrote, "The world moves faster and faster; and the new difference will probably be considerably greater. The temper of each new generation is a continual surprise", which seems a good point to leave behind the Industrial Revolution and move on to today. The foregoing has been but a selective view of an important period in time regarding the understanding of Globalization, solely intended for the present study. Because of the similarities in aims and purpose; the historical "baggage" that the West and especially non-Western societies are left with as a result of the Industrial Revolution; and an understanding of the huge upheaval experienced at the time, I feel that it provides an essential introduction to Globalization. Understanding something of the Industrial Revolution is I think important in beginning to understand the development of "us" and "them" which continues to have an effect on current relations. It also seems to provide the sort of model that Globalization is based on or is what Globalization has inevitably become.

Before leaving the Industrial Revolution, we might ask how that experience still affects the relatedness of members of those non-Western societies whose way of life was destroyed. It is sometimes easier to reflect on our own bad experiences rather than trying to understand the bad experience of others that we have responsibility for: especially others that we treated as barbarians. If we reflect on the system of political relatedness at the international level between Britain and France we can see the way that past events have the effect of long-lasting, still strongly held attitudes and stereotypes that considerably affect and hinder the development of current relationships. At this level of relatedness we have very little in common, we have been in a position of fierce competition for centuries and this continues as a potential for disaster in relationships between French and Britons. If we likewise reflect on the system of political relatedness at the international level between the West and Russia we can also see the way that past events of the Cold War results in mutually strongly held attitudes and stereotypes that affect and hinder development of current relationships.

A highly significant aspect of an understanding of this period is in regard to relatedness. The Industrial Revolution had a major impact on the whole way of life for many societies throughout the world. The working and living conditions of the "working class" in Britain and other Western countries were such as to promote disease and illness; while for those in other countries their fate was to be regarded as Barbarians and their known way of life destroyed. The Industrial Revolution transformed the entire world. It took the form of a European expansion in and conquest of the rest of the world. The memories, attitudes and stereotypes developed out of the experiences of that time are bound to have a significant mutual influence on both Western and non-Western societies and a political system of relatedness at the inter-cultural level is bound to be a significant factor in any inter-cultural experience. Such is the similarity and the highly emotional effects of the Industrial Revolution that the current experiences are bound to evoke experiences of the former period. A result may be that members of each respective culture may be viewing today's experiences from extremely different perspectives. As such there is a considerable opportunity for disaster.

And now let me turn to the current Globalization. It would seem that Globalization is producing societal dynamics that are every bit as all-pervasive and far-reaching as the Industrial Revolution. And we shall see that now, as then, it is not just a matter of a change in our technology, or an economic process, but a change in our whole way of life.

CHAPTER FOUR

Globalization

I n this chapter I shall attempt to provide an explanation of the way that the process of Globalization is manifesting itself in the world today. Rather like the Industrial Revolution, what we refer to as Globalization is a largely imperceptible phenomenon. I wish I could say that I will start with something as conventional as a definition of Globalization. Sadly, I cannot. No such definition exists. However, I will try to provide a view of what Globalization is all about and what it seeks to achieve that has been developed from multiple sources. We can say with some degree of confidence that starting in about 1985 a dramatic and growing change started to roll out across the globe and that this was strongly driven by the implementation and availability of the www. As with the Industrial Revolution, it was not just the change in technology, but the fact that the new technology has brought into being a new way of living. Globalization, like its forerunner, was originally driven by economic need but has developed way beyond that to begin the process of creating in societies throughout the world a new way of life. At this time, what that new way of life will be is not known and we are currently at the stage where we are experiencing "death of a known way of life".

Origins of Globalization

As was said in the last chapter, international rivalry especially war, tests the resources of a state as nothing else does. When they cannot pass the economic test, they crumble and fall, as was the case with France at the time of the Industrial Revolution. One major rivalry dominated the world scene for most of the twentieth century, and lay at the core of its recurrent periods of general war. This was a costly and highly competitive era ferociously fought between two different philosophies that eventually resulted in the fall of the Soviet Union and of Communism. Doubtless there were many contributing factors for this outcome but high among them must have been finance. Trying to match the military spending of the West finally brought about an end to communist ambitions. As was shown in the last chapter, a near identical situation existed in the period before the Industrial Revolution. As then in regard to Britain, so now, with regard to the USA which was left without serious competition and able to pursue a global initiative.

Without doubt this was a significant outcome but it will be helpful to gain a wider appreciation of the context in which Globalization came to dominate. During the 1970s the world had slipped into a depression. Instead of action world leaders embraced reaction by concentrating on the management of what they insisted was a recession. But then there was another recession, followed by another and another one after that. The conditions pertaining at the time included an energy crisis, followed by inflation, unemployment, economic stall, debt, more inflation, unemployment and so on. It was described by Governments as a sequential recession, but never as a depression. This was almost certainly because if there were a depression there would also have been the need for a major leadership failure, as well as an urgent need for dramatic leadership initiatives. A recession on the other hand was something managers could handle because the broader forces were not assumed to be out of control. The notion that scientific management could deal with any problem was rife.

In the Preface reference was made to problems arising from a rational approach that excluded thoughts about societal culture and human emotions which inevitably have an impact on societies as a whole. The above actions of world leaders are similar to those referred to earlier and reflect the management approach taught on MBA courses that supports the Globalization project. During this period, and indeed still continuing today, there was a succession of management books that sought to document the latest quick fix: the current fad. Seen from a rational economic perspective that sort of statement seems to make sense. However, it is to ignore the irrational that exists in all societies which are largely and mainly concerned with issues of culture. A scientific, business case approach that ignores emotional and cultural aspects is simply a denial of organizations and societies as processes of human behaviour.

Out of these crises came a terrifying combination of inflation and depression. It was called stagflation. All of this together produced a sense of powerlessness among the elites, which they communicated instinctually and even openly to the members of their societies. And this was followed by a stock market crash in 1987. Clearly, some large scale response was needed that would enable Western economies to produce the income necessary for the maintenance of a modern society. A combination of factors, not least the technological revolution that brought us electronic mail (email) and the www, provided the conditions for Globalization to be developed. Other factors such as the retreat from Soviet style Communism in 1989, as well as important changes in political spheres such as eased Government restrictions on capitalist activities in China, Vietnam, and Cuba, all contributed by providing an environment that would enable Globalization to develop.

It seems highly likely that the twenty-first century could well be the "global century", even if the rapid Globalization of people, products, and markets slows from its current blazing pace. Increasingly, organizational participants are being urged to "act global, think local" or to become part of the "global village", but definitions, descriptions, and visions of Globalization vary widely, making it quite difficult to know what it means to be "global". Additionally, it is not at all clear what the costs and benefits of Globalization are or are likely to be for the future. To begin to clarify some of the issues it might be helpful to ask, what is Globalization? A common response is that Globalization can mean many things to many people. For example, Jan Pieterse (1995) asserts that, "there are almost as many conceptualizations of Globalization as there are disciplines in the social sciences. For purposes of exploring the concept of Globalization it is broadly defined as increased permeability of traditional boundaries of almost every kind, including physical borders such as time and space, nation states and economies, industries and organizations and less tangible borders such as cultural norms or assumptions about how we do things around here." This is supported by Parker (1998), who states that "The world increasingly resembles a global marketplace where integration across 'traditional' boundaries is evident in almost every dimension of life. The daily news demonstrates growing worldwide integration across boundaries like time or national borders that once seemed immutable, and in academic fields the boundaries between disciplines like management, finance, marketing and other fields have also become more fluid."

Characteristics of Globalization

A summary of the characteristics of Globalization by various authors provides the following view: Globalization looks at the whole world as being nationless and borderless; Goods, capital, and people have to be moving freely; The global enterprise is less place bound and less tied to the traditions of a single nation; The break with national traditions can result from geographic separation that occurs when a firm operates largely outside national borders; Boundary permeability or transcendence; High rate of change; A growing number and diversity of participants; and Rising complexity and uncertainty. These are all principal features of Globalization and the stated aims were for goods, capital and people to be moving freely in a nationless and borderless world. However, that was to ignore the need for members of the various societies for the continuity, consistency and confirmation of their world that Kernberg (1966) refers to, which was provided, in large part, by their societal cultures. If the possessions and roles by which we gain our continuity, consistency and confirmation are experienced as being chaotic, then we can assume that if we lose our ability to predict and to act appropriately, our world will begin to crumble, and since our view of our self is inextricably mixed up with our view of the world, that too will begin to crumble.

Behind the notion of Globalization was the belief that trade would lead to growth, international relations, to democracy, to almost anything. It was as if trade had become the engine of the world, a panacea for all problems. It was an attempt to simultaneously reshape economic, political and social landscapes. And if economics and technology are seen to be the great inevitable forces of today, then management is to be seen as more like a support system that makes the other two seem inevitable. The abrupt rise to hyper-respectability of management schools and their linking with large corporations led by technocrats has had an astonishing effect of confusing management with leadership. And this in turn leads to the wonderfully unaccountable belief that if leadership is reduced to management, well then, problems are not to be solved: they are to be managed. Business, political and social leaders would believe that they are in fact no longer problems. As stated earlier, this is a rational approach devoid of almost any human science considerations.

Global structures

Like the Industrial Revolution before it, Globalization did not burst out of the gate in the early 1970s. It would be a good fifteen years before people felt they knew what they meant when they said the word. These fifteen years were filled with attempts to define the international prism with treaties, the handling of crises, and forma-tion of international organizations: the development of a whole new structure that would in general operate over and above the existing national and international structures. For example the World Trade Organization (WTO), the 1995 successor to the General Agreement on Tariffs and Trade (GATT), is a worldwide membership organiza-tion (127 members) established for the purpose of defining world-wide commercial relationships. As was the formation of G8 where Government leaders of the world's most powerful democracies were trumping existing international gatherings by creating a more senior structure and one dedicated to looking at the world through an economic prism: Other organizations include Trade Alliances such as the European Union (EU), the Organization of Petroleum

Exporting Countries (OPEC), the North American Free Trade Agreement (NAFTA), the Asian Pacific Economic Cooperation (APEC); as well as Inter-governmental Cooperative Agreements, such as the Organization for Economic Cooperation and Development (OECD); and Non-governmental Organizations (NGOs), the latter primarily being voluntary groups organized to address concerns viewed as low priorities among governments and most businesses but also shaping economic and political interests. Some examples are: Save the Whale, Amnesty International, Human Rights Watch, and Medicine Sans Frontiers.

The World Bank, the United Nations, and the International Monetary Fund were all set up in about 1947 in the aftermath of two World Wars in an attempt to influence political, social and economic activity throughout the world. At that stage the needs of poor countries was not really an issue and the intent was to promote trade and arbitrate disputes at a global level. Mainly Western nations used the processes to rebuild after the war and subsequently remained in economic control of Asia, Africa and Latin America. This resulted in a half century of unfairness in the global trade system. Globalization has raised awareness of the status of these and other more recent Global institutions. It is an interesting thought that these institutions that possess considerable power and influence are to all intents and purpose outside the democratic process. The World Trade Organization is a closed shop and appears to be acting as a defender of its members. It aggressively dismantled the barriers against trade in industrial goods and services that benefited its members. But at this time it is working to prevent free trade in the area of agriculture and textiles which is where poor countries can compete. At a time when "democracy" is promoted by Western countries as the panacea for all world problems, this would seem a considerable contradiction.

The vehicles for achieving the aim of Globalization are the transnational companies that are seen to be at the cutting edge of the market's leadership of Globalization. It was suggested that they would become like virtual states and their aggressive dominance would make them impervious to local political prejudices. As with the new structures these new style organizations were set up in a way that they also would be acting largely outside the restrictions imposed by national law. An interesting thought comes to mind in regard to the procedures currently employed by the USA in regard to terrorist prisoners. Could it be that Globalization was the model on which Guantanamo Bay and other facilities were based beyond the national law? The growth of multi-national organizations meant that some had greater income generation and were more powerful than many nation states. It was considered that the power of the nation state would wane and that such states as we know them might even die. In the future power will lie with global markets, thus economics not politics and armies will shape human events. The promise of Globalization went as follows: The global markets freed of narrow national interests and regulatory constraints, will gradually establish international economic balances; And, so we will have at last outgrown the eternal problem of boom-and-bust cycles. Such markets will unleash waves of trade. And these waves will in turn unleash a broad economic tide of growth. That tidal wave will in turn raise all ships, including those of the poor, whether in the West or in the developing world.

The idea was that it would enable us to take advantage of the technical and theoretical breakthroughs. The result would be a growth of wealth and general well being through a multiplication of players, situations and factors. From which it was concluded that all of the foregoing would create the conditions for healthy governance, which would result in the emergence of debt-free governments. It was a strongly held belief that the market would stand for no less. In short, it was posited that freed from the fetters of wilful men, we will be able to follow our individual self interests toward a life of prosperity and general happiness. The high point of Globalization came in 1995 with the creation of the WTO. This included a secondary triumph, the inclusion of intellectual property in the WTO's responsibilities. The collection of royalties was now to be treated as an item of trade.

Beyond economics

There are clear indications that the development of a new way of life is a clear political aim of some in the West. However, it also seems the case that nations experiencing rapid economic growth have inevitably faced an equally rapid demand to adapt their social, political, legal and other systems. Just as the Industrial Revolution resulted in movement of people from rural areas to the newly formed cities so we have seen similar activity within countries such as China. In addition, we have seen immigration across national boundaries. There is a considerable debate as to how far Globalization can go in terms of changing the world. Some would have it that it is possible, in terms of either common habit or business-inspired materialism, to create a truly global culture. As was stated in the Preface, the view taken here is that those who believe that this is possible are deluding themselves by ignoring the influence of societal cultures.

As an economic model the intentions that "Globalization looks at the world as being nationless and borderless" and "goods, capital and people have to be moving freely", may make economic sense. To be able to move manufacturing processes to the area of the world that can provide the cheapest materials and labour could be of benefit to all involved, although the experience of the Industrial Revolution has shown that the exploitation of cheap labour produces harsh working and living conditions. The question that needs to be asked, though, is whether the notion of a "borderless, nationless world where people can move freely" is the considered and agreed policy of Western governments. Every single Western society is experiencing "death of a way of life" and this is frequently expressed as having been "invaded" and their culture and identity destroyed. They are suddenly living in a society that has no discernible identity and they respond by a mixture of dependency and violent rebellion. A familiar position as you will recall from the last chapter.

As with the Industrial Revolution there are two aspects of Globalization. On the one hand, there are the economic benefits of new technology and economic processes; on the other, there are the effects of these processes. The latter seems to be conveniently ignored by most people for most of the time. If we reflect on the Industrial Revolution we will recall that the experience then of "death of a way of life" was to evoke dependency and violent rebellion. As will be shown later in this chapter, dependency is demonstrated through religion. Violent behaviour is demonstrated in various Western and non-Western societies in a way that shows that it is ever present beneath the surface. A classic example is the way that following what might be regarded by many as a relatively minor incident, the publication in Denmark of a cartoon insulting the Prophet Mohammed, rioting quickly broke out in Western and non-Western societies. As was previously stated messing with culture is a dangerous practice.

There are two aspects arising from the free movement of people. On the one hand is the movement of people in their own countries that seems to replicate the processes and experiences that were occurring during the period of the Industrial Revolution. On the other hand, there is the movement of people to other countries and other different societies. Immigration is occurring on a mammoth scale and every Western country now has large numbers of immigrants living and sometimes working in those countries. The question that arises is whether it is the policy of Western governments to allow large scale immigration. If it is not, then we might further ask how does a security conscious Western nation like the USA which has twelve million illegal immigrants, and Britain which has about half a million illegal immigrants, justify their lax security. It would appear that by taking a non-position enables Western governments, on the one hand, to enjoy the advantages of cheap migrant labour while the immigrants remain dependent, compliant and out of the public view. But on the other hand they are still able to claim they are illegal and subject to "transportation" back to their country of origin if they become rebellious by adopting any form of anti-social behaviour. Again, it all sounds very familiar.

In summary Globalization is seen as an inevitable form of internationalization in which cultures are reformed from the perspective of economic leadership. The leadership here is provided not by people but by the innate forces of economics at work; that is—the marketplace. But as was the experience of the Industrial Revolution, the intentions were not simply economics. It was also considered that the resulting prosperity would allow perceived oppressed members of societies to convert dictatorships into democracies. But of course these democracies would not have the absolute powers of the old nation states. And so we would see a shrivelling away of irresponsible nationalism, racism, and political violence. It was also seen that on the economic front, the very size of the new markets would require even larger corporations. And their size will raise them above the risks of bankruptcy. A result being that this produces a further source of internal stability.

Democratization of the world

That the intentions were not simply economic but went much further than this by an intention to change the world is confirmed by the following quotations that provide us with an insight to the political intentions for Globalization: Alfred Eckes, Chair of the US International Trade Commission described it as "a process in which technology, economics, business, communication and even politics dissolve the barriers of time and space that once separated a people". Anne Krueger, Number two at the International Monetary Fund described Globalization as: "all leading to the closer integration of the world including—but not limited to—economics". Thomas Friedman of the New York Times described Globalization as "the inexorable integration of markets, nation states, and technologies to a degree never witnessed before". Even from a Western perspective these are, to say the least, grandiose ideas that seem beyond belief.

These sorts of statements are typical of monocular notions of Western supremacy. There is not the slightest hint that there has been any consideration of the position of non-Western societies whatsoever. It is a simple, rational statement of what will be good for one and all in purely economic terms. It follows the pattern of the Industrial Revolution whereby attempts were made to make the "other", wherever he or she was located, more "like us". Then the principle means of achieving the aim was "religion". It would seem that the current principle means is "democracy". Neither religion nor democracy is bad *per se*, on the contrary both are admirable aims. But when, as happened in the Industrial Revolution, religion was thrust upon members of non-Western societies whether they wanted it or not, sometimes at the point of a gun, and when democracy is thrust upon a non-Western society (Iraq) whether they want it or not, at the point of a gun, it raises contradictory messages. The aim in Iraq appears to be that of creating an autonomous state capable of managing its own affairs free of the previous tyrannical regime. However the process of insisting on democratic government is like saying "we are going to empower you". A result is continuing dependence on the West. In reality the West cannot empower them, they can only empower themselves. You can be sure that the message is not lost on other non-Western societies throughout the world.

Not surprisingly, some see the project as nothing less than an attempt to control the world. They are doubtless encouraged by statements that promote the wide ranging political intentions of Globalization as described by President Clinton as "The enlargement of democracy" and by President Bush as "Beyond containment lies democracy", and when referring to its mission to "be the promotion and consolidation of democracy". To a lesser degree and in less obvious ways this is also the aim of the European Union. Various authors have voiced concern about the New World Order version of Globalization. The main concern is that it can become a new name for imperialism as stronger economic entities use their economic clout to exact concessions from weaker entities, whether they be workers, other companies or even nations. The threatened 1995 trade war between Japan and the USA represented this form of imperialism with the US bullying Japan until it showed favour to US exporters, particularly auto exporters. By the same token China has threatened to close its markets to the US if the latter assists Taiwan with political memberships, and still other nations rule out trade relationships with firms based in countries that have staked out territories as "enemies". Globalization ideals are considered to represent primarily Western perspectives.

Recent events that are seen to be contrary to the concept of open borders and free trade have concerned restrictions by the European Union to limit the supply of goods from China. The availability of such goods being seen as a threat to the existence of traditional national industries throughout the European Union. A further event has concerned the ownership of P&O, recently sold by its UK owners to a company in Bahrain. So far so good, but one part of P&O concerned the port security at Baltimore in the USA and therefore Congress vetoed foreign (Muslim) ownership on the grounds of national security. At the time of writing Ministers from developing countries were said to be set to clash with their European and American counterparts at an emergency summit of the WTO aimed at preventing key talks on Globalization being compromised by a recent rise in protectionism. The fear was for thousands of jobs and billions of pounds of revenue being lost in the developing world.

Given the fears expressed in the preceding paragraph it is perhaps not surprising that, of today, efforts to achieve the wider aims of controlling the world through Globalization have met with limited success. Part of the thinking is that it is possible to change the culture of the world by a number of low-level factors. A number of activities have been identified as sort of initiators that will lead to Globalization of culture. First, it is considered that products ranging from cola beverages to denim blue jeans that are consumed throughout the world will affect the culture. The view put is that many of these products attract the global teenager market that adopts the same modes of dress, jargon, music, entertainment preferences, and even converging values for environmental stewardship. A further strand of the argument is that English is increasingly used as a business language, being spread via internet and tourism and many forms of mass entertainment. In other words, it is seriously considered that it is possible to achieve a truly global culture through the processes of a mixture of common habit and business-inspired materialism.

I have to say that this is simplistic rubbish and shows little understanding of the nature of societal culture. The mistake is to mix popular culture with societal culture. As stated in the Preface, many serious attempts to change culture in organizations, a far simpler process than that of changing societal culture, fail. The very nature of culture, organizational or societal, means that it is within us all. Or put another way, we are societal culture. Simply changing our taste in terms of clothes, beverage or television viewing will not change societal cultures. On the contrary, it is just as likely to be seen as a threat to the societal culture. Almost all non-Western societies are resistant to this pressure from the West. And by far the greatest resistance is that of Islamic and Asian societies.

Of considerable influence on Globalization is the internet and www. An essential feature of free trade is a free network yet there has developed a significant view that large communications and entertainment organizations such as Microsoft, Murdoch, CNN and Google are gradually getting control over the network. Internet freedom, like freedom of trade, is espoused and great play is made of Chinese attempts to control email content; an activity that would appear to be more for political purposes than for trade and business. However, I am sure we are not naive enough to think that in the West the internet is free of monitoring by security services and perhaps others, in the same way that telecommunications is monitored. The possibility of controlling the actual means of communication, as opposed to what is delivered on it, is one of the oldest managerial dreams, stretching back through all empires and religious systems. Here you see the national and historic link between absolutist leadership and controlling management. It is central to the idea of monopoly and oligopoly and whether real or phantasy is bound to raise fears of a new form of imperialism or economic colonization.

Western governments have seemingly been surprised that Globalization has not been emphatically endorsed by nations across the globe. Rather it has resulted in increased Nationalism in Europe and elsewhere. And the resurgence of Islam, as was the experience at the time of the Industrial Revolution, seems to have been something of a shock. At the heart of the problem lies the globalist idea of viewing society through an economic prism. In simple terms this has meant demoting ethical and moral values of society in favour of the certainty that humans are primarily driven by self-interest. The thinking goes along the lines that they will not mind being confused with machines, provided their income is raised. It would be difficult to find a clearer example of the self-delusion of Globalization theories. Far from being impressed with the globalist idea, members of societies have adopted forms of behaviour that they feel are appropriate under the circumstances imposed upon them by their environment. This behaviour has frequently been a rejection of Western culture and ideology.

We see then that Globalization, far from being an economic process, is (as was the Industrial Revolution) a full blooded attempt to change other cultures and Nation States by imposing Western standards, philosophy and culture on them. In effect, it is an attempt to provide a one-world scenario where all live in the same way. If we need to be convinced that this is not feasible or desirable the history of the Industrial Revolution and recent history provides us with a wealth of evidence. For all the benefits of the Industrial Revolution the most outstanding feature was the effects of these processes that eventually dominated the outcomes. The effects of the processes of the Industrial Revolution resulted in a long and sometimes violent struggle by non-Western societies for autonomy that eventually resulted in independence and freedom to control their own destinies. Recent history demonstrates this strong desire of societies throughout the world to move from dependency to autonomy. It seems foolish that the West should embark on a further process that ignores the historical consequences.

What seems certain is that Globalization will, as was the case with its forerunner the Industrial Revolution, continue for some considerable time and will not come to an end but will become the accepted, recognized and developed way of doing things. For most people in both Western and non-Western societies there is an awareness that they are living through a period of profound change but are unable to be more specific. Ultimately the effects of the processes of Globalization will be the most outstanding feature. How long will this situation continue? Can history point us in the direction? In regards to other aspects of Globalization the Industrial Revolution provides very helpful comparisons, the first Globalization lasted for nearly seventy years. At a guess, I would suggest we have at least another ten years to go before things settle down. As will be seen in the next chapter, the effects of Globalization are experienced by people in many societies as highly intrusive and painful. Such is the nature of change that their known world has been destroyed under their feet and adjusting to this situation results in feelings of powerlessness and hopelessness. How they react is key to understanding current societal dynamics.

In the following two chapters I shall try to analyse and reveal something of the consequences of Globalization. My starting point in the next chapter is the effect of Globalization on Western societies.

CHAPTER FIVE

The effect of Globalization on Western societies

I n this chapter I shall provide the first of two analyses concerning the effects of Globalization, starting here with the effect of Globalization on Western societies. The main source for this analysis will be the findings of OPUS Listening Posts that were referred to in Chapter One. Such is the dynamic nature of the process of Globalization that the changes are largely imperceptible and the more traditional research methods are not at all helpful. A result is that other than in the most general sense, there really is little other material available. Perhaps if we take the nature of Globalization as being "revolutionary" we might ask the following sort of questions: "when you're in the middle of a revolution how do you know where you are going? When you are subject to revolutionary change how do you analyse it? When everything is in a state of flux how do you analyse it?"

It may be of interest that some of the Listening Post Reports referred to the fact that "the intellectuals have disappeared from the public scene", the view is that they are not contributing and it would appear that they are as helpless as others. We might hypothesise that intellectual activity and understanding relates to "known" information; whereas here we are concerned with a totally new way of life that is in the process of development and is information of an "unknown" quality. In addition, there are few signs that individuals or those responsible for the management, leadership, and administration of political, economic and social institutions currently have the ability to adopt the required reflective approach that will help to make sense of this (still developing) "new way of life". Given such a background, OPUS, and their associates throughout the world, through its attempts to encourage the reflective citizen, is one of the few research organizations capable of helping to provide a serious understanding of these seemingly inexplicable societal dynamics.

In early January of 2004, 2005 and 2006, under the guidance and coordination of OPUS, International Listening Post Projects were held in multiple countries with the aim of providing a snapshot of the societal dynamics of each country at the dawn of those years. These were all reported in a similar format, researched, and analysed by OPUS personnel, to produce a Global Report. The aim was to identify major or dominant themes arising within the Reports of the countries involved; to analyse and collate supporting information from the Reports; and to formulate hypotheses arising therefrom. For current purposes a much abbreviated version of the Reports will be used to show the way that Globalization has affected the mainly Western participating countries. An added advantage is that by moving through the three-year period from 2004 to 2006 it will be possible to see how things have been changing over that period.

Global dynamics at the dawn of 2004

In January 2004, Listening Posts were held in thirteen different countries around the world (Australia, Canada, France, Germany, Britain, Holland, Ireland, Israel, Italy, South Africa, Spain, Sweden and the USA). Four major themes were identified as being common to all or most countries. These are: (1) Globalization; (2) Loss of institutional authority; (3) Death of a way of life; and, (4) The creation of an individualistic response.

It seems appropriate that the first Theme is "Globalization". Here the analysis based on the National Reports showed that:

There is considerable information in the National Reports to support the notion that Globalization is having a major impact on all participating countries.

This led to the hypothesis that:

There would appear to be no escape from the effects of Globalization in any of the participating countries. Globalization is experienced as persuasive, intrusive and all encompassing. Such is the extent and depth of change arising from Globalization that many experience their society as having been "invaded". An outcome is that members of societies are left without the ability to comprehend what is happening in their environment. Left feeling helpless, angry and utterly confused the anxiety is such that they respond by using defence mechanisms such as denial, displacement and rationalization. Frequently, they are left in a paranoid schizoid state where primitive splitting and projections onto governments or other institutions (labeled the Welfare State) are mixed with strong desires for dependency from these same governments and institutions.

Under the second Theme, "Loss of institutional authority", the analysis showed that:

National Reports identified a theme of disillusionment or loss of trust in traditional institutions—the church, politicians, police, health authorities, education system, and others. These institutions had previously provided a sense of identity and containment. The reported experience now was that they not only did not provide containment but they added to the feelings of fragmentation, uncertainty and fear.

This led to the hypothesis that:

Social institutions, often identified with the welfare state, faced with a rapidly changing environment have found it difficult to transform themselves in an appropriate way. The response is either to employ old and (previously) trusted methods that are now inappropriate or to impose strategies which amount to centralized control. A result is that institutions that were once treated as containers of good and bad aspects of the self, are now felt to be failing. They are experienced as being unreliable, and dependency is exposed. Individuals feel lost, overwhelmed, fragmented and disillusioned becaue they have fewer external sources of dependency. This loss is experienced as the loss of a source of identity and social cohesion. Members of society react to their anxiety whereby reality is denied and transformed into something less severe or projected onto others. Rather than face up to the difficult task presented they prefer so split off, and project the bad things onto other institutions—the church, politicians, police, health authorities, and others.

Under the third Theme, "Death of a way of life", the analysis showed that:

> Several National reports identified this theme with only minor variations, summed up by a statement in the United States report, "It ain't what it used to be". Others alluded to it in more general ways. There was a widespread view that, what can only be referred to as a "revolutionary" social change, has left people (perhaps older people in particular) struggling—and frequently failing—to make sense of a much changed world.

This analysis led to the hypothesis that:

> The reported experience regarding the nature of social change is such that one can only conclude that it is in the nature of a "revolution". The depth and quality of change that causes members of society to refer to feelings of de-Christianization, dehumanization and a loss of known values, "an unravelling of the social threads that have held us together", can only be regarded as "the death of a way of life". Under pressure from this rapid social change, undoubtedly influenced by global technological advances and a resulting information explosion, individuals have felt increasingly exposed, confused and dislocated. The resulting unbearable complexity of change is much too difficult to bear and members of society adopt a defence against the anxiety by way of denial and a form of flight into phantasies of a lost idealized past that almost certainly never existed.

Under the fourth Theme, "Citizenship—the creation of an individualistic response", the analysis showed that:

> The sort of words or phrases which were repeatedly used in the National Reports to describe the experience of citizenship in the various locations were as follows: "insecurity", "impotence", "help-

lessness", "hopelessness", fragmentation", "an inability to think", "information overload", "disintegration", "withdrawal", "rage", "paralysis", "individualism" and "a need to validate self". This resulted in a sort of withdrawal into the self.

This led to the hypothesis that:

Faced with the loss of so many familiar "good" and "bad" societal objects, members of the various societies are left having to take back their "good" and "bad" projections. An outcome is that they experience their environment as fragmented and they in turn are left feeling insecure and helpless as individuals. On previous occasions, they would have known from whom and where they might find validation of their thinking. Faced with previously unknown experiences they have no previous experience to compare this perceptual data with. They therefore need to engage in "new" thinking. The difficulty arises when they turn to those same other members of society to validate their "new" thoughts and are rejected. Others are also in the same boat, as it were, and all are trying to make sense of this new environment, consequently, they are also having different "new" thoughts. It is therefore akin to the Tower of Babel—many voices, none making sense to the other. The ensuing feelings of helplessness lead us to adopt a defence against action and engagement. A result is that members of society withdraw, turn inwards and seek solace in their own private world. Thus is created the individualistic attitude and approach that dominates societies around the world.

Other themes were also identified as follows:

Generational Issues: Several of the National Reports referred to generational issues. We did not see this as a stand-alone issue. Rather, it was seen as a reflection or consequence of the other themes identified above. Thus, references to generational matters were seen as a defence against anxiety whereby, the helplessness of the older generation is dealt with by vesting all hope in the younger generation; or, the younger generation is used by the older generation as a scapegoat and the blame for all that is wrong in society is displaced onto the young generation.

Third World: Again, several of the National reports refer to the Third World. We are aware that all Reports are from the Western world or Western influenced countries and that none are from the so-called Third World. These references would indicate that the Third World was very much in the mind of those participating. However, we would suggest that this also be seen as a defence against anxiety by way of an identification with Third World citizens by those who are also helpless and unable to influence.

Under Concluding Remarks, the Report stated:

There can be little doubt that globally we live in interesting and stressful times. We therefore wanted to conclude on a constructive and more positive note. We do so by quoting the following Hypothesis from the German Report:

To approach all this we shall have to learn to endure irreconcilable tension between our current ideals and reality. Both idealization and demonization of politicians and other responsible figures are mere projections that have to be withdrawn in order to develop personal responsible activity. This functions only where we develop awareness of the consequences of what we ourselves perform. This is insolubly connected to opening up emotional involvement. To develop and conserve this quality of being alive we require emotional space where experience is possible without pressure. This appeared to be the pre-requisite to facing change and thus assume a counterpart position to despair and helplessness: a counterpart that must be perpetually fought for and renewed. [Stapley & Collie 2004]

Global dynamics at the dawn of 2005

In January 2005, Listening Posts were held in fifteen different countries around the world (Australia, Bulgaria, Chile, Finland, Germany, Holland, Ireland, Israel, Italy, Serbia, South Africa, Spain, Sweden, USA and Britain). On this occasion two major themes were identified as being common to all or most countries. Theme One, "Monumental Social Change", which has four sub-themes as follows: (a) Helplessness and powerlessness: withdrawal from global to local; (b) The search for scapegoats and saviours; (c) Incapacitated, political economic and social institutions; and (d) Disintegration of society and individualistic retreat. Theme Two is The Asian Tsunami disaster.

By way of introduction to Theme One, "Monumental Social Change", the Report stated:

> For some while now the world has experienced an unprecedented and revolutionary social change that has shown no signs of relenting. Rather, the pace and intensity of change appears to be deepening and intensifying. The nature of the change is so all-encompassing that it has been referred to as "death of a way of life". Largely inspired and driven by Globalization it has left individuals, and those responsible for the management, leadership and administration of political, economic and social institutions in a state of bewilderment. They are seemingly unable to make sense of this "new way of life". So far-reaching is the change that in many instances individuals and groups simply have no previous knowledge as points of reference, and therefore no language, to express their experiences. It is as if they are on a journey without a map or language to guide them. Or as the Italian Listening Post suggested: "The metaphor of being on a journey at sea was put forward to describe the experience of having left the security of a well known port and being in the middle of the ocean, not yet at the new destination that, incidentally, we do not know."

> Not surprisingly, current global dynamics are mainly concerned with the anxiety, frustration, anger, rage and feelings of hopelessness arising from loss and failure to cope with a "new way of life". All National Reports strongly identified with the notion that social change was of such intensity that it was experienced as bewilderment. This is a complicated and complex situation. However, we have identified three distinct ways that societies respond and react to the anxieties arising from the changes experienced and these are documented below as sub-themes. Although formulated as three distinct sub-themes it should be borne in mind that they share the same basic foundation—they all emanate out of the monumental social change that is occurring across the world.

Under the first sub-theme, "Helplessness and powerlessness: withdrawal from global to local", the analysis showed that:

> Faced with the extreme anxiety arising out of the circumstances described above, members of society throughout the world are left with an inability to make sense of what is going on. It seems clear that

Globalization is experienced as playing a highly significant part in all national matters, leading to feelings of bewilderment in the face of complexity. In many of the reports, these experiences were associated with a desire to withdraw to family and neighbourhood. Issues such as the war in Iraq and multi-nationals, all have an immense impact on national elections and other activities, as does the fear of global warming, aids and other natural phenomena.

This led to the hypothesis that:

Because of the intense anxiety arising out of the "loss of a way of life" and attempts to make sense of and adapt to a "new way of life", the impact leaves individuals throughout the world feeling confused, guilty, vulnerable and despairing. As society becomes more difficult to understand throughout the world, so we find our ability to think about the meaning of social processes is diminished. There is a sense of not knowing where we fit in to this new and ever-shifting reality. As a result we seek to defend ourselves from the anxieties associated with this uncertainty by retreating into the local—neighbourhood, friends and family—where we hope we can make sense of reality and act effectively. Insofar as this is a flight mechanism it will not be successful, and will inhibit the need to develop new ways of reflecting, new ways of being creative and active in the world.

Under the second sub-theme, "The search for scapegoats and saviours", the analysis showed that:

Faced with the extreme anxiety arising out of the circumstances described above, members of societies around the world make use of familiar and known objects such as the old and young; male and female; and unknown objects such as immigrants, fundamentalists, and other "different" people to help them cope with the discomfort experienced. Because this anxiety is evoked at a deep level, members of society feel overwhelmed, and this arouses paranoid schizoid defensive behaviour. They do so either by creating scapegoats who are used as vehicles for bad projections; or by creating saviours who are used as vehicles for good projections. In some case such as the young they may be used for both purposes.

There is a natural envy of youth which coupled with doubts by the older generation about the sort of legacy they will leave, makes young people a ready vehicle for projections. In one respect, the young are at an advantage as they are able to have some understanding of current dynamics. They have less previous internalized knowledge and feelings and are therefore more able to assimilate new information. This is not the case with the older generation who are much less likely to make sense of current dynamics. They have a great deal of internalized information and feelings and therefore if they are to make sense of this new information there is an inevitable and considerable loss.

It would appear that faced with a highly challenging and seemingly inexplicable environment, we seek explanations in knowledge that we can have a degree of certainty will be shared by others. We revert to notions of the family and more especially to notions of male and female roles in society and question whether political correctness has in some way been responsible for the circumstances leading to "not knowing". We also indulge in blaming the unknown other: those such as immigrants, fundamentalists, "them", "different" people, are all blamed and used as convenient scapegoats for our discomfort and "not knowing".

This led to the hypothesis that:

Because of the intense anxiety arising out of the "loss of a way of life" and attempts to make sense of and adapt to a "new way of life", members of societies throughout the world experience massive anxiety which is evoked at a deep and primitive level, they feel overwhelmed and this arouses paranoid schizoid defensive behaviour. As a result members of societies engage in splitting by creating good and bad objects as vehicles for their projections. Known and familiar objects in the shape of young and old; male and female are more likely to be used for positive projections; and the unknown other in the shape of immigrants, fundamentalist and "different" others are more likely to be used as repositories for negative projections. The nature of projections is to idealise and create good objects that will prove saviours; or to denigrate and create bad objects that can be used as scapegoats for all ills.

Under the third sub-theme, "Incapacitated political, economic and social institutions", the analysis showed that:

Faced with the extreme anxiety arising out of the circumstances described above, those responsible for the management, leadership and administration of political, economic and social institutions throughout the world are in a state of bewilderment. They are seemingly unable to make sense of this "new way of life". So far reaching are the changes that in many instances individuals and groups simply have no previous knowledge, and therefore no language, to express their experiences. A result is that institutions are not just failing they are incapable of dealing with today's changed needs.

One of the ways that institutional leaders deal with "not knowing" is to develop simplistic initiatives and to trumpet them as a sort of "cover up" for what is really happening. The other side of this is the way that members of society engage in serious "splitting" and the use of mainly negative projections into institutions as a defence against not being able to understand. Faced with the difficulty of "not knowing" what the real problem is but also being the recipient of massive projections to "do something", a frequent and totally inappropriate response is for politicians and other social leaders to impose "tick-a-box" controls.

This led to the following hypothesis:

Because of the intense anxiety arising out of the "loss of a way of life" and attempts to make sense of and adapt to a "new way of life", those responsible for the management, leadership and administration of political, economic and social institutions throughout the world find it impossible to know with any certainty what is going on; there is no "right" response when faced with such complexity. At the same time, politicians and policy makers are forced to act, as people put projections of competence into them, thereby rendering themselves infantilized and impotent. Leaders, who take on the projected expectations of omnipotence and omniscience in the paranoid schizoid position, fail to go through the proper process of honest consultation, instead taking the path of power by stealth. They also devise a proliferation of catchall measures of accountability as a defence against the risk associated with uncertainty. A result is that the controls not only diminish risk but also lock out creative potential: the capacity for thought and deliberation, the toleration of difference and exploration in the face of change. This is seen as an abuse of authority by the Government-appointed Regulators and Inspectors, who ignore the formal authority of the managers they are regulating or inspecting. This results in a distrust of current leaders.

Under the fourth sub-theme, "Disintegration of society and individualistic retreat", the analysis showed that:

> Faced with the extreme anxiety arising out of the circumstances described above and especially dynamics arising out of Globalization members of societies throughout the world have experienced serious effects on social relationships. Economic migration has had the effect of massive movement of large sections of the population throughout the world. This has had an effect on both the host nation and the families of those who are left in the country of departure. Changes in work practices and other social changes have had the effect of weakening family stability. At a different level, many are in a position of not being able to communicate with others because we can no longer be sure that other individual members or groups in society share "taken for granted" views. A result is that rather than get into difficulty when we attempt to test our reality with these others we retreat into individualistic action.

This led to the following hypothesis:

> Because of the intense anxiety arising out of the "loss of a way of life" and attempts to make sense to and adapt to a "new way of life", this has aroused fears of personal safety and even annihilation in individual members of society. A result is that they have been increasingly driven towards taking an independent approach. However, our sense of self depends on validation of others and we cannot exist solely as independent beings, we can only be dependent if we are interdependent. A result is a breakdown of internal defences and increased internal anxiety which is acted out with a result that society is experienced as an unintegrated environment.

Under Theme Two, "The Asian Tsunami Disaster", the analysis showed that:

> Nearly all National Reports directly or indirectly reflected this major natural disaster. At one level, it was such a tragic and massive social event that hardly anyone could not be affected by it. At another level, this tragedy provided an outlet for many psychological experiences

around the world, and for images that expressed responses to wider social processes. Faced with the extreme anxiety arising out of the circumstances described in Theme One above, feelings of being overwhelmed by bewildering societal changes, of social structures being swept away, of guilt and reparation were all connected to both the tsunami and global processes.

This led to the following hypothesis:

The tsunami is both a disaster in the external world, and a metaphor for internal, unconscious experiences of wider global forces, and how they impact on societies and individual citizens. In particular, feelings of being overwhelmed or flooded by rapid and bewildering social change, and resulting feelings of guilt and helplessness, have close associations with the overwhelming response to the tsunami. The opportunity to respond actively and positively to a known external disaster is in contrast to, and provides relief from, a growing sense of alienation and inner turmoil in the face of Globalization and loss of familiar social reference points. The Tsunami provides an opportunity to displace feelings of personal victimization onto victims of the disaster. In addition it would seem to provide an outlet for giving which can be benevolent but can also be seen as influenced by a darker more evil motivation designed to cover our feelings of guilt by paying off those who we have treated badly. Or at another more primitive level it may be seen as an attempt to pay off the Gods for their anger at our actions.

Under Concluding Remarks, the Report stated:

Everything points to the possibility that current global dynamics will continue to intensify and deepen in the foreseeable future—or perhaps, to be more accurate, that should read unforeseeable future! Given that there are few signs that individuals or those responsible for the management, leadership, and administration of political, economic and social institutions currently have the ability to adopt the required reflective approach that will help to make sense of this, still developing "new way of life", there is not much hope of serious understanding. As referred to in some of the National Reports, "the intellectuals" have disappeared from the public scene, they are not contributing and it would appear that they are as helpless as others. It would seem, then, that global dynamics will continue to be dominated by defences against anxiety. (Stapley & Collie, 2005)

Global dynamics at the dawn of 2006

In January 2006, Listening Posts were held in twenty-two different countries around the world (Australia, Bulgaria, Canada, Chile, Denmark, Finland, France, Germany, Greece, Holland, Ireland, Israel, Italy, Mexico, Norway, Portugal, Russia, South Africa, Spain, Sweden, USA and Britain). On this occasion two major themes were identified as being common to all or most countries. Theme One, "Coping with Continuing Social Change", has three sub-themes as follows: (a) Loss of identity; (b) Failing paternalistic leadership; (c) Splitting, displacement and scapegoating of the "Other". Theme Two is "Attempting to understand change—a virtual or phantasy environment".

By way of introduction the Report stated:

> As was the experience in the last two years, the world is going through a period of unprecedented and revolutionary social change that still shows no signs of relenting. The nature of the change, which was referred to as "death of a way of life" in 2004, is still powerful and influential at both a social and a psychological level in all societies. The effect of Globalization has been such that it has impacted upon all aspects of society be that individuals or those responsible for the management, leadership and administration of political, economic and social institutions. Members of society in all countries are struggling to come to terms with these changes and the current social dynamics are in large part evidence of the ways that members of societies are developing means of coping. There is little if any evidence to show that any particular society has started to come to terms with a "new way of life". Indeed, the evidence is to the contrary. The National Reports provide a picture of a world that is experienced as one of total confusion and inexplicable dynamics, which results in frustration and increasing rage at the extreme impotence experienced by members of societies. Given these circumstances, and indicative of the extreme anxiety being experienced, the means of coping are, in the main, primitive responses based on splitting and projection.

By way of introduction to Theme One, "Coping with continuing social change", the Report states:

> All National Reports related to the ways that members of societies

throughout the world were developing a means of coping with the anxiety, frustration, anger, rage and feelings of helplessness and powerlessness that were arising from loss and a failure to cope with a way of life that is experienced as threatening their very identity. This is a complicated and complex situation, however, we have identified three distinct ways that societies respond and react to the anxieties arising from the changes experienced and these are documented below as sub-themes. Although formulated as three distinct sub-themes it should be borne in mind that they share the same basic foundation—they all emanate out of the continuing revolutionary changes that are occurring across the world.

Under the first sub-theme, "Loss of Identity", the analysis shows that:

There is considerable evidence in the National Reports to conclude that the changes in societies around the world are so dramatic and so destructive that individuals and groups are experiencing a loss of identity. This dire experience is described by Winnicott as, "Integration feels sane, and it feels mad to be losing integration that has been acquired"; and by Melanie Klein as, "One of the main factors underlying the need for integration is the individual's feeling that integration implies being alive, loving and being loved by the internal and external good object; that is to say, there exists a close link between integration and object-relations. Conversely the feeling of chaos, of disintegration, of lacking emotions, as a result of splitting, I take to be closely related to the fear of death". It seems little wonder therefore that members of society should describe their experience as "death of a way of life".

This led to the following hypothesis:

Members of societies throughout the world continue to experience their societies as totally dynamic processes that exist in a state of flux and are characterized by spontaneity, experience, conflict and movement. Such an environment is deeply disturbing not the least because it does not provide the continuity, consistency and confirmation of our world that we require. A result is that members of societies are left with a serious threat to and loss of their identities. This results in a struggle for independence and at times a regression to a primary identity. The overriding effect is a retreat into individualism and isolation, which in turn means that society becomes even more fragmented. The chaos and madness that ensues out of disintegration is a highly dangerous situation that may literally result in members of societies acting as if the other is totally bad and deserving of whatever fate he or she might be considered to merit.

Under the second sub-theme, "Failing paternalistic leadership", the analysis showed that:

The mainly patriarchal leadership is identified by members of societies throughout the world, with a failure to provide containment. A result is that members of societies seek alternative forms of leadership. There is a great deal of evidence in the National Reports to show that the old paternalistic, controlling, model of leadership that has prevailed in most political, economic and social institutions, especially religious institutions, has been seen to be ineffective, inauthentic, and failing to provide containment. In effect, it has been seen to be unsuitable for today's needs and has been largely rejected. However, this has resulted in members of societies throughout the world having to take back their dependency needs. Being left with no obvious location for their projections, this results in an experience of helplessness, powerlessness, frustration and anger. In some societies they have located their dependency needs in women who have been mobilized to take up leadership roles, resulting in matriarchal leadership both at a societal and family level. In other societies dependency needs have been located in young people who have been mobilized as fight leaders to express the frustration, rage and anger on behalf of societies.

This led to the hypothesis that:

The effect of Globalization has been such that it has impacted on all members of society including those responsible for the management, leadership and administration of political, economic and social institutions. In common with others, societal leaders have also been exposed to complex dynamics and would appear to have suffered the same anxieties and helplessness. Perhaps we should not be surprised that they have also found great difficulty in providing adequate responses to the many complicated problems they have been required to deal with. However, for members of society this "inadequate response" has been experienced as a failure to provide adequate containment. Feeling helpless and without any means of making sense of their experiences, members of societies search for alternative forms of leadership. The extreme dependency, which was located with the societal leaders, is now located back with the members of societies and this is dealt with in various ways. The most obvious available leaders are women who are regarded as offering a more reflective leadership. This may prove so in some instances but in other instances it may be simply idealization and Basic Assumption leadership that is being mobilized. A more worrying way that dependency needs are being displaced is in regard to young people. It would appear that there is a view that young people are able to cope with the modern world better than older people. This can lead to an unconscious displacement of dependency needs onto young people and a subsequent mobilization of young people as fight leaders.

Under the third sub-theme, "Splitting, displacement and scapegoating of the 'Other' ", the analysis showed that:

Globalization is experienced by society as an all powerful and controlling influence that creates a sort of alternative world that is experienced as a tyrannical monster, which is driven by economic policy with its own value systems. A result is that those responsible for the management, leadership and administration of political, economic and social institutions adapt these values which turn our institutions and organizations into the same tyrannical monsters. Members of society are left with feelings of powerlessness and an inability to control and influence their lives. A typical response is as contained in the Australian Report, "Much of the discussion around this theme had a 'paranoid tinge' with feelings of anxiety and fear. This was particularly so in relation to the accessibility of private information and to the powers held by the 'authorities' in regard to detaining people. It was linked to the question of who can we trust?" At these times of increased uncertainty members of societies throughout the world identify a convenient "other" to act as a repository or scapegoat into which they can displace all their hateful and malicious feelings. The "other" in many countries is immigrants, especially Muslim immigrants, who are part of their societies; or are identified terrorists in other countries. But in some countries the "other" may be polarized political parties. Having a common enemy enables members of societies to suppress their own guilt and to assert their rights to preserve a common identity. However, a result is polarization and the development of fixed and inflexible notions about this "other", which results in demonization. A further result may be that the "other" acts on the projections of demonization and becomes what the members of society are seeking them to be.

This led to the hypothesis that:

Members of societies experience a high degree of anxiety, not least that arising from the loss of identity. In societies throughout the world, there is a strong sense of uncertainty about socially acceptable behaviour, norms and values. They are unable to classify their experience on any basis of similarity and are unable to make sense of their experiences. It is a kaleidoscopic world with few if any reference points. The uniqueness of the here and now is intolerable. The personal and social boundaries are blurred and there is no consensus as to what is acceptable or not acceptable. A result is that members of societies experience anxiety at a level that is unbearable and splitting and projection are used to find comfort. For many, the means of coping is to project the rage associated with helplessness into an "other". In many instances, the "other" is located in those who are clearly identifiable as different from ourselves: in most situations this will be immigrants and in many situations Muslim immigrants, who are experienced as the most different and in some instances associated with terrorism. The "other" may also be terrorists in other countries or even Globalization itself. In some instances it is internal splitting and polarization that produces the "other" for each party, which seems to be exemplified by the dynamics in the USA. A danger is that polarization in all circumstances produces a rigid "other" for each party. This then leads to confrontation based on relatedness rather than reality.

Under Theme Two, "Attempting to understand change—a virtual or phantasy environment", the analysis showed that:

All National Reports related to the way that members of societies were beginning to question and to try to develop explanations for the way that specific societal changes have affected members of society. Although not clearly understood, members of societies throughout the world are realizing that Globalization and technology have had distinct effects, which seen in the kindest light can be seen as bewildering and surrounded in puzzlement and mystery, and seen in the harshest light can be seen as potentially harmful and destructive to the future of societies. In many countries there was a strong theme of concerns about communication and of the means of communication. There is a growing realization that there is a real issue about how you communicate with others in a world that is full of new means of communication. As in Theme 1 above, this is a complicated issue that is inextricably linked to the changes within societies and responses by members of societies.

This led to the hypothesis that:

The impact of Globalization results in members of societies experiencing a lack of control over their environment and a feeling of deprivation at a psychological level. A result is that members of societies utilize multiple means of communication as a defense against isolation and lack of attachment. Such however, is the nature of this communication that it only leads to a sort of virtual world where members of society share the illusion that anything is possible, denying the reality that true relationships are not achieved. Members of society are still left feeling isolated, impotent, dehumanized and remain psychologically deprived.

Under Concluding Remarks, the Report stated:

As will have been seen from the extracts of National Reports above, for members of societies to stay in the depressive position is a mammoth and at times near impossible task. Yet the Listening Posts show that reflection does lead to the possibilities of thoughtful dialogue when members of societies are able to suggest possible ways forward. An example is the following extract from the Danish Report: "Ambivalence, feelings of guilt, muddled sensations and frustrated energy could be interpreted as a potential for political action directed at defending civic rights for all, for an involvement in real exchange between ethnic groups, for working with what it means both to be a world citizen and a citizen in a nation and a local community. (Events since the Listening Post was held, have demonstrated just how difficult these issues are.)

Given that there are still few signs that individuals or those responsible for the management, leadership and administration of political, economic and social institutions currently have the ability to adopt the required reflective approach that will help to make sense of this, still developing 'new way of life', there is not much hope of serious understanding. Everything, therefore, points to the possibility that current global dynamics will continue to intensify and deepen in the foreseeable future. This is a potentially worrying time, the feelings and emotions associated with a loss of identity and a reliance on the 'other' as a means of coping with the extreme anxiety experienced, could make it likely that many societies will be faced with dangerous and violent conflicts in the coming year.

Whether the likely shift from paternalistic to maternalistic leadership will provide the necessary reflective stance or be experienced as equally impotent, remains to be seen. However, the biggest danger lies in members of societies unconsciously mobilizing young people to provide for their dependency needs. Faced with such strong feelings of helplessness and having a captive audience in the family, expressed concerns and impotence can easily be unconsciously conveyed as the seeking of a saviour; and that young people are mobilized to fill that saviour role" (Stapley & Cave, 2006).

One way of thinking about the above is to view it from the perspective of societal culture. In doing so we might first think about the way that out of the interrelatedness of the members of societies with their notion of "society in the mind" which is developed from their perception of the societal (holding) environment, a societal culture or way of life is developed that provides for the human need for consistency, continuity and confirmation. This process occurs in every society throughout the world and because of the unique membership of the society and their unique environment they produce a unique culture. However, no matter that the cultures have differences they still have the same purpose: that of providing forms of behaviour that the members of the society feel are psychologically advantageous to them under the circumstances imposed upon them by their societal environment. In doing so this results in a societal culture that will provide containment such as we have needed from birth onwards. That does not mean that society is a static unchanging phenomenon, on the contrary, it is a dynamic process that is constantly changing albeit for most of the time imperceptibly. For many years, probably since the period of the Industrial Revolution, Western cultures have evolved in a continuous and developmental manner with the dynamic processes arising steadily and gradually over many years.

However, when we think about the above analysis of the effect of Globalization on Western societies we can see that something profound is happening and that the dynamic processes are of such an intensity and frequency that the consistency, continuity and confirmation normally part of our societal culture is fragmented and non-existent. Life as we knew it no longer exists, we are living in a period of history that is experiencing "death of a way of life". This is a world that makes little sense to members of Western societies and one that is experienced as being out of control. Members of Western societies experience fear, rage, impotence, vulnerability and despair; they experience a lack of containment, social disintegration, uncertainty and insecurity; and this even extends to fears for personal safety and annihilation, and threats to and loss of identity.

The ways that members of Western societies have responded have been remarkably similar to the way that those who were alive during the period of the Industrial Revolution responded then: by dependency and violent rebellion. Dependency is shown in several different ways: Displacing dependency onto political and religious leaders; A flight into an independent approach; Regression to primary identities; Denial and flight into own private world—resulting in an individualistic attitude which dominates Western society; The projection of hope and fear into the younger generation; A search for the magical; and A phantasy that a Messiah will rescue them. Violent rebellion is also shown in several different ways: Displacement of fear and rage projected into identifiable groups such as immigrants, asylum seekers and Muslims, who become the bad object and are then demonized; Demonization of bombers leading to stereotyping and scapegoating of Muslims; Projection of rage and hurt into marginalized groups that we then perceive as Barbarians; Splitting and locating evil and hatred in the powerful (usually USA). I think you will agree that this is a picture of a society that is beyond comprehension and is highly disturbing at both a social and psychological level which at times leaves members of society witless.

At the social and political levels some results have been as follows. Leaders have been used by societies as a whole as vehicles for their projections. Many of these projections—at least in the earlier days, were highly seductive and difficult, being of a highly positive nature which sought to idealise leaders who would lead them to a promised land free of anxiety—as would any Messiah. Perhaps not surprisingly this had the effect of creating omnipotent leaders who thought that they could do anything. Subsequently members of societies seeing their dependency needs fail began to express their anger at their leaders. The leaders for their part realized that they had to do something but were as impotent as the rest of society, so they simply implemented policies that were "smokescreens to cover inactivity". Many of these resulted in greater controls over members of society. But the greatest concern is that regarding the effect on the young who have been mobilized to provide hope and to take the blame. One effect of putting reliance on youth is that they make take the authority given without having the experience to do so.

Having seen something of the dramatic effect that Globalization is having on Western society I shall now turn to an analysis of the effects on non-Western societies. We don't have the benefit of Listening Posts in those countries but we can be sure that the current societal dynamics in the West will be replicated in at least equal measure in Muslim and other societies.

CHAPTER SIX

An analysis of the effects of Globalization on non-Western societies

An old saying informs us that "you can take the American out of America but you can't take America out of the American". Put another way, American culture is part of every American and it will travel with him or her no matter where they go. And it is thus for Chinese, Africans, Muslims and Indians. Their cultures will all be different but whatever their culture members of those societies will take their unique culture with them as part of their identity. This of course has considerable implications for immigrants living in a different society. Whatever society we may be a part of wherever that may be in the world, the process of cultural development is the same. Members of society interrelate with their societal environment and develop forms of behaviour that they feel are psychologically appropriate to them under the circumstances that they perceive are imposed upon them by their environment. However, being a unique society and a unique environment, each society will develop a unique and different culture. In certain circumstances, some facets of this culture may be shared by other societies. For example, European national cultures have some similarities but all are in total very different and unique.

Understanding difference

In thinking about non-Western societies we need to consider that the similarities are likely to be less and the differences likely to be more when compared with Western cultures. Each of those societies has a history, tradition, and culture that is exceedingly different to Western societies. I start this chapter, then, with a simple acknowledgement that members of other non-Western societies are different and as such the effect of Globalization on those societies is also likely to be different. I don't doubt that Globalization will still be experienced as "death of a way of life" but we are referring to a different way of life and therefore the response may be different from those of Western societies.

This chapter, while referring to all non-Western societies, will nevertheless make particular reference to Muslim societies. Industrialization has an effect on societies in China, India and other Asian societies, where there appears to be an embracing of aspects of Globalization, and this will be referred to. However, in following the aim of this book to understand the connection between Globalization and terrorism, the predominant problem of this time, we need to carefully consider the effect of Globalization on Muslim societies. We can helpfully start with the unremarkable observation that members of Western societies and members of Muslim societies are the most different "other", for each other at this time. There is currently a mutual lack of knowledge or state of ignorance that exists between members of Western and Muslim societies. This is a dangerous position to be starting from as it raises primitive fears for both Muslims and Westerners. Being the most different "other" for each other also raises the likelihood that each will use the other to stress the badness that they are not. Relatedness based on attitudes and stereotypes developed from past experiences may result in mutual feelings and phantasies about the other. We may expect, therefore, several versions of reality from both sides.

Given the extreme emotion that terrorist actions arouse in all of us it is not unnatural that we should entertain feelings of hatred and disgust; and that we should have strong needs for some sort of revenge. We could be forgiven for thinking that civilized people would not do this sort of thing; but from this position it is then an easy step to the stereotyping of whole groups of people as Barbarians. Such is the emotional turmoil that we demonize and treat as inhuman those we "know" are responsible. To even attempt to put ourselves in the shoes of members of other Muslim societies then becomes near impossible. This is not the sort of information that we find easy to listen to. In like manner, I find it difficult to listen to suicide bombers but as in organizations. When we listen to the "rebel leader", the one who is seen as a nuisance, we are listening to the only one who is telling us what the other members of the organization are saying behind closed doors. One of the London suicide bombers Mohammed Khan said "Your democratically elected governments continuously perpetuate atrocities against my people all over the world . . . Until we feel security, you (the West) will be our targets." This is difficult to hear but it is likely that he is telling us what the members of Muslim society, including those that are part of British society, are saying behind closed doors and difficult as it is we need to listen.

To fully understand the effect of Globalization on non-Western societies we need to try to see things from this other perspective: we need to try and stand in the shoes of members of non-Western societies. And by taking an empathetic stance, try to understand their experiences and emotions. This is far from easy, not least because we first have to deal with our own relatedness which for many of us has resulted in an underlying distrust between Western and other non-Western societies which is partially based on reality but is also greatly influenced by large doses of phantasy and feelings arising from within us. Frequently, these are feelings of hatred and vengeance that we do not want to own and therefore dispense with them by projecting them onto convenient others. This convenient "other" is more often than not those who are most different and about whom we have little real understanding. Being seen as so different we fail to see them as fellow human beings who share all of our goodness and badness, stereotyping them only in regard to their badness. In these circumstances we cannot begin to be empathetic. So the starting point is to see Muslim and other non-Western societies to be the same as us, but as having different experiences and perceiving some things in ways different from us.

If you were born in a part of the world that is a non-Western society reality will be different than for us born in a Western society.

What is not different is that we, and they, are all human beings who are capable of both goodness and badness. However this is frequently ignored because the West has had a major and at times devastating impact on almost every non-Western society. Not least as a result of their actions during the period that we have referred to as the Industrial Revolution. The relation between the power and culture of the West and the power and culture of other societies, is, as a result, the most pervasive of all conflicts. If we reflect on the Industrial Revolution we may conclude that the West won the world not by the superiority of ideas or values or religion, to which few members of other societies were converted, but rather by a total approach that included its superiority in applying military action and might. Westerners often forget this fact or rationalize our good intentions; non-Westerners never do. As victors we are liable to forget many things. As victims we seldom ever forget anything and I have little doubt that members of Muslim and other non-Western societies who remember and refer back to the Industrial Revolution will hold the view that colonialization tried to deform their cultural traditions. For members of Muslim societies the experience will have been seen as an attempt to destroy the cultural traditions of Islam. Thus to take a view that the conflict is at the level of religion is only partially correct. To be accurate, the conflict is to be regarded at a higher level, one of conflicting cultures. The relatedness, or mutual influence of Western and non-Western societies has a long history that impacts upon today's reality as experienced by both societies.

"Us" and "them"

One of the basic arguments of this book is the idea that we can view societies or cultures as intelligible fields of study. And that these can be studied in the same sort of way that we use to study other sized groups. Basic to this way of thinking is our individual need to classify and categorize sense data and to create boundaries. From this process we can develop an important notion of what is "me" and what is "not me". And this extends to group thinking whereby we classify what is "us" and what is "not us". The largest groups are societal or cultural groups and where differences result in conflictual and abrasive interfaces or boundaries we may see conflict on an inter-cultural scale. The relations between the great religions of Islam and Christianity have frequently been stormy. And such are the different realities that the other has almost continually acted as the "other" for each. More often than not the relation has been one of intense rivalry and of varying degrees of hot war. Efforts by the West to universalize its own values and institutions, to maintain its military and economic superiority, and to intervene in conflicts in the Muslim world generate intense resentment among Muslims. For example, the long-standing political and military arrangements between the United States and Saudi Arabia in regard to the exploration and marketing of oil has almost certainly been resented by other Muslim societies. And as we saw in regard to the brief history of Al Qaeda the decision to rely upon the might of Western military forces to free Kuwait from the invasion of Saddam Hussein was even more resented.

It is against this background that we can begin to consider the effects of Globalization on Muslim and other non-Western societies. Sadly, at this time, there are no Listening Posts held in Muslim or for that matter other non-Western countries. However, it may be reasonably considered that if the effect of Globalization on Western countries throughout the world is so emphatic it is far from unreasonable to assume that the effect on non-Western societies is at least equal if not greater. When we see the turmoil that is occurring in Western societies, not least the view that what is occurring is "death of a way of life", and that members of societies are left in a state of disintegration that threatens their very identity, we can but appreciate that something significant and profound is happening. It seems most likely that Muslim and other non-Western societies will also be affected by the significant changes taking place across the world.

Social conditions

As a sort of rough guide to the way that non-Western societies experience Globalization we can also set it in the context of the impact that the first Globalization had on both the Western and the non-

Western worlds. There are three particular areas that we may helpfully consider: social conditions, industrialization, and religion. In regard to the former, we may recall that in the first Globalization the effect of movement from the country to the inadequate towns in Britain and other Western countries meant that many workers were deprived of the traditional institutions and guides to behaviour. A result being that many sunk into an abyss of hand to mouth expedients and mass alcoholism was an almost invariable companion of the headlong and uncontrolled industrialization and urban spread.

For what was then movement to urban living in the West, today we need to refer to movement from society to society: global immigration. For many immigrants the experience is similar to that of Western workers at the time of the Industrial Revolution. It is a removal from traditional institutions and guides to behaviour into inadequate housing and other social conditions. Cut off from the usual strong family ties and controlling institutions of their own societies and cultures they find themselves in a liberal society where seemingly anything goes. Threats to and loss of identity for individuals and groups will doubtless be highly stressful. For members of Western societies in the Industrial Revolution the stress resulted in mass alcoholism and rebellion. For today's immigrants I feel sure that the experience is equally stressful and the recent experiences of rioting Muslim youths in France show that rebellion is ever present beneath the surface and can easily erupt into actual civil disturbance including rioting. I fear that this is a phenomenon that we shall experience in many societies.

But there is another important aspect—that concerning the impact of Globalization and immigration on those members of non-Western societies who remain at home while their, mainly young, family members emigrate to foreign lands and foreign cultures. In many instances this will raise fears of their loved ones living in what they will regard as a decadent society. The reported experiences of immigrants, such as poor housing, lack of employment opportunities, and suspicious or racist attitudes of the host society, may only serve to reinforce their picture of the West. And this is likely to be further reinforced by the development of communication facilities around the world. There can be little doubt that one of the most important contemporary manifestations of Western power is global communications. The ready availability and low cost of the use of the visual media and the internet undoubtedly had a part to play in the defeat by the West of Communism. In like manner, it is currently being used on the global stage with many, mainly American, multinational media organizations transmitting twenty-four hours a day programming throughout the world. However, as was the experience of the first Globalization, others very quickly copy developed processes. Thus we have the Arabic multi-national media organization Al Jazeera broadcasting to the world as does CNN or other Western media organization. In addition, Al Qaeda and other terrorist organizations have also understood the value of visual communication and are ensuring that terrorist acts are televised and made available to the Western and other media.

As regards the material that is beamed into the homes in non-Western societies, while it was anticipated that this would have a positive effect and encourage a democratic approach, these may have a more negative effect than was anticipated. By way of example, Western liberal broadcasts which show women enjoying their normal Western rights and members of Western societies enjoying freedom of speech are selectively used to display decadence and Western anti-governmental views. Broadcasts that show the Western way of life are used in non-Western societies to denounce Western cultural imperialism and to rally the members of those societies to preserve the survival and integrity of their indigenous culture. The extent to which global communications are dominated by the West is thus a major source of the resentment and hostility of non-Western peoples against the West.

Industrialization

For some, such as China, the experience has been the same as it was for British workers at the time of the first Globalization. Here they have simply moved from their own countryside to the growing cities where they can engage in the industrial employment supporting Globalization. As was the case with the textile factories in England, so now the condition of factories in China leave much to be desired. Most of the workers have to move far away from their families. The men and women employed in the factories are working ten-hour days for six days a week and most live with five or six others in rooms that have no electricity or running water. Sometimes it's a fight to get paid. In comparison with the Industrial Revolution these are still early days in the process of Globalization. However, if we are to learn from that experience we can predict that at some stage these workers may also rebel and that they will also fight for the development of a Chartist type mass labour movement.

Others in non-Western societies who are not directly engaged in the industrial processes are also subject to the cultural changes that Globalization brings to their societies. As was the case in the first Globalization, new technology (machinery as it was then) was one of the chief benefits to be expected from private enterprise and free competition. But the resistance to this "new way of life" was expressed not only by the labouring Luddites who arose to smash the machinery, it was also supported by the smaller businessmen and farmers in their regions who sympathized with them because they also regarded innovators as destroyers of men's livelihood. In China, a similar situation seems to be occurring where farmers are fighting to retain their land for agricultural purposes against the wishes of local and central governments who wish to build factories on the land. As then, the alternative to escape or defeat is rebellion. And such is the situation of the farming poor that we begin to see the appearance of labour and socialist movements and of social revolution.

There can be little doubt that Globalization has increased the intrusion of the West into the Muslim way of life at both the social and technological levels and this has almost certainly caused greater turmoil than that described regarding Western societies. However, it is at the religious level that we really see the effects of Globalization. Given that the Muslim world is subject to Sharia law and to religious control it is not surprising that religion should be the area most affected. It will be recalled that in the first Globalization one of the most significant outcomes was the increase in religious activity. In the West the increase was not in the established churches but in the evangelical religions such as Methodism. Highly significant was the fact that this was also the period of the greatest increase in Islam and perhaps equally significant is the current increase in evangelical religion in the USA.

Religion

Of all consequences arising from the Industrial Revolution, the effect on religion is vital to our understanding of today. During the period of the Industrial Revolution (as now) there was a considerable increase in religious activity and a considerable change in the sort of religions that were being followed. I believe this is symptomatic of the degree of upheaval in societies arising out of the effects of Globalization. For most members of societies anywhere, religion is part of our internalized values and beliefs not to mention our conscience. Each of us develops our own set of values. By means of the primitive process of introjection we take in values that then form internal mental images which become part of our stock of knowledge.

It is this sort of knowledge that the rational, economic approach to Globalization has ignored. But of course, truth is, we cannot ignore what is part of every member of society, in every society throughout the world. When the way of life that each and every one of us has helped to create is torn apart and the culture that we relied upon for containment destroyed we are likely to respond in a dependent manner or we rebel, if needs be using violence. Both responses are important as a means of understanding the current global dynamics. I earlier referred to dependency as a response to extreme anxiety both in regard to the Industrial Revolution and regarding current experiences. The nature of that dependency is born of helplessness and hopelessness resulting from a fragmented and destroyed culture whereby members of Western societies experience death of a way of life and seek relief from whatever source they feel may help. This includes magical thinking that they can find a Messiah who will deliver them from this unbearable experience.

This is the experience in all Western societies, but in America in particular the response of turning to evangelical religion appears to be much stronger than in other societies. Relating to this experience Krantz (2006) offered some observations about the growing embrace of religious sensibilities across the social and political spectrum in America. He explains that, "a re-enchantment of the world can be evidenced in many ways. To name but a few: widespread embrace of non-institutional spirituality; growing interest in astrology and other occult disciplines; and burgeoning growth of non-traditional churches." He continues, "Mature religious sensibilities have often found expression in institutional religion, which has provided a home for uncertainty and a source of ethical meaning. Yet mainstream congregations in the USA have shrunk sharply in recent years while evangelical and fundamentalist churches have grown dramatically. It is on this part of the spectrum that I want to focus because it is on Evangelicalism and Fundamentalism that leadership is being conferred today. There can be little doubt that a new religious feeling is growing in our culture, frightening in its paranoid-schizoid qualities with sharp splitting between love and hate, good and evil, the righteous and sinners. . . . Large parts of our population, overwhelmed by anxiety, abandonment and loss are asking God to bring order to internal disarray."

In times of rapid social change established identities dissolve, the self must be redefined, and new identities created. For people facing the need to determine Who am I? Where do I belong? religion provides compelling answers, and religious groups provide small social communities to replace those lost through urbanization. In this Globalization a most striking development in the West has been the incredible growth of evangelical churches, especially in the United States. And as Krantz informs us, in 2003 alone $1.7 billion was spent on evangelical books in the United States. For all Americans religion has become an increasingly important aspect of life including political life. At the same time we have seen a huge increase in the interest and growth of Islam in the Muslim societies. Given the understanding of the first Globalization and the effect of the current Globalization on Western societies where the "death of a way of life" has led to a search for a Messiah, we may then begin to understand the resurgence of Islamic religion.

The most obvious, most salient and most powerful cause of the global resurgence of religion is precisely what was thought would cause the death of religion: the processes of social, economic, and cultural modernization that have swept across the world that we refer to as Globalization. As we have seen, long-standing sources of identity and systems of authority are disrupted; people move from the countryside to the city; become separated from their roots; and have taken new jobs or have no job. Those that have emigrated interact with large numbers of strangers and are exposed to new sets of relationships. They need new sources of identity, new forms of stable community, and new sets of moral precepts to provide them with a sense of meaning and purpose. Evangelical and fundamentalist religion meets these needs.

Some presumed effects

Comparisons from the period of the Industrial Revolution and the known effects of the current Globalization show that in all likelihood the effects on non-Western societies are going to be much the same as the effects on Western societies as detailed in the last chapter. At this point it may be helpful to refer to some of those specific effects and to apply them to non-Western societies. In the 2004 Global Report it was stated that, "Such is the extent and depth of change arising from Globalization that many experience their society as having been invaded." There is some support for this in regard to the references to the intrusive nature of communications referred to above. In Western societies this perceived invasion of society was responded to by a mixture of blaming their own internal others such as political leaders and dependency on those leaders. In Muslim societies it would appear that the response is one of anger and blaming external others such as the USA and President Bush. Leading from the perceived death of a way of life members of Western societies struggled with the problem of lack of reference points by withdrawing into individualistic retreat. It would seem that the Muslim response to this same experience was again one of fight, and of anger addressed to Western societies and Western leaders. In other words the experience is the same but the perceived threat is external rather than internal.

Also in 2004 it was stated that members of societies referred to experiences of de-Christianization, de-humanization and a loss of known values that was regarded as "death of a way of life". The Western response was again one of dependency on political and other societal leaders but when this was seen to have failed, members of Western societies sought scapegoats and stereotyped all Muslims as bombers. If Muslim societies had such an experience it is not difficult to see how they would have responded in a dependent manner by seeking the required consistency, confirmation and continuity in Islam. The fact that there has been a massive increase in the support for Islam can be seen as confirmation of the Muslim experience that follows the experience of the Industrial Revolution, which also led to a rapid expansion of Islam. Allied to an experience of death of a way of life is the issue of the mobilization of youth. In the West, youth were seen to be used both to blame and to provide hope. It seems that the response in Muslim societies was to mobilize the young to carry the fight to the West.

In the 2005 Global Report it was stated that, "current global dynamics are mainly concerned with the anxiety, frustration, anger, rage and feelings of hopelessness arising from loss and failure to cope with a new way of life. . . . Global issues such as the war in Iraq and multi-national companies were all adding to a sense of inability to think and make sense of our experience." Here we see the way that matters outside societal boundaries can impact on our way of life in a highly disturbing manner. In the West the discomfort was dealt with by retreating into individualization. Faced with the same experience it seems more likely that members of Muslim societies will have turned to Islam to provide a sense of attachment to known and trusted figures and processes. In Britain, at this time, there was a suggestion that some members of society finding many of their identities hard to confirm, were turning to primary identities such as a religious identity where they knew that centuries old traditions would provide them with containment. This would almost certainly seem to be the case with members of Muslim societies.

Also in 2005 the experience in Western societies was one of extreme anxiety that resulted in the search for scapegoats and saviours. In the West the scapegoats were seen as immigrants, fundamentalists and "different" others who were all used as repositories for negative projections. It seems certain that faced with the same dynamics the Muslim response would be the same except that in this instance the repositories of negative projections would be those of Western origin: the killers of innocent Iraqi's, the great Infidel that is the United States of America, and Bush, Blair and other Western leaders who are seen to be instrumental in promoting and leading the processes of Globalization that is invading Muslim societies. The saviours in the West were seen to be the young and sometimes females. It seems likely that given similar experiences those in Muslim societies also see their saviours as the young people. We perhaps have a confirmation of this in the way that Muslim youth was mobilized in France to protest against the poor social and employment conditions of Muslim immigrants.

In the 2006 Global report it was stated that, "the changes in societies around the world are so dramatic and so destructive that individuals and groups are experiencing a loss of identity". This was viewed as reinforcing the notion of the "other" being a totally and wholly bad object that was unable to be seen as good in any possible way, and deserving of whatever fate he or she might be considered to merit. Here we can see members of Western societies who are experiencing feelings of disintegration and chaos lashing out at those who they have classified as evil to such a degree that they don't care what happens to them. If this is also the experience of members of Muslim societies we can expect a further hardening of their attitude to the bad objects that they identify as the West, Western values, and Western leaders. Thus we may at this most dangerous of times be in danger of both cultures being full of hatred for the mutual "other". The 2006 Report added to references in the previous two about the dangers of all societies mobilizing young people to provide for their dependency needs. It is feared that the dangers of extreme dependency on young people as a result of a wish for a saviour is that young people would be mobilized to fill that saviour role by taking the fight to the mutual "other".

Other non-Western societies

Related but different causes lie behind the challenges of non-Western societies. The economic development of China and other Asian societies provides their governments with both the incentives and the resources to become more demanding in their dealing with other countries. Muslim assertiveness can be seen to stem from social mobilization and population growth. In particular the expansion of the 15–24 year old cohort in Muslim societies, that age group who may most likely be attracted to the rebellion and the glory of terror or the challenges of migration. This may be true, but there is another aspect to this which is also significant, that concerning the way that young people are mobilized to do something on behalf of society. Doubtless, the experience of Globalization in Muslim societies is similar to that in Western societies where members of societies experience helplessness, powerlessness and become dependent. In their dependent state they project their hopes and needs for rescue into young people. A result, as in France and Australia, is that young people are mobilized to lead the violent rebellion. In much the same way, Muslim youth are mobilized to lead the violent rebellion through the medium of suicide bombings and other terrorist actions.

Economic growth strengthens Asian governments, and this is particularly true of India and China. An effect of the Industrial Revolution was that others societies took on the processes and imitated the successes of the West, learning and copying from Western example. This appears to be the case with China who are currently building alliances with oil rich African and South American countries which in turn is causing Western governments to become increasingly concerned about losing control of this essential commodity. China has risen to be one of the biggest economies in the world and is anticipated to grow to be the biggest within a decade or so. In recent years there have been signs that the Chinese are developing similar approaches to those adopted by the West. Their ability to produce cheap goods of high quality is already threatening traditional producers in Western countries who are responding by adopting protectionist measures that of course are contrary to the aims of Globalization. Each of these challenges, Asian economic strength and Muslim population growth, is having and will continue to have a highly destabilizing effect on Western global politics.

While Asians become more assertive as a result of economic development, Muslims in massive numbers are simultaneously turning towards Islam as a source of identity; meaning, stability, legitimacy, development, power, and hope; hope epitomized in the slogan "Islam is the solution". When we reflect on the experience of Western societies that are having to somehow come to terms with feelings of loss of identity and of feelings of disintegration which is experienced as chaos and a near death experience, it may be no wonder that Muslims are turning to religion. Following the Islamic resurgence in the first Globalization, this resurgence in its extent and profundity may be seen as the latest phase in the adjustment of

Islamic culture to the West. It is an effort to find the "solution" not in Western ideologies but in Islam. It embodies acceptance of modernity, rejection of Western culture, and recommitment to Islam as the guide to life in the modern world.

Some Westerners including President Clinton, President Bush and Prime Minister Blair have argued that the West does not have problems with Islam but only with violent Islamist extremists. This seems to be a belief based solely on a monocular Western perspective. A view that seeks to deny the magnitude of the problem by attempting to reduce it to a "manageable" proportion: one that permits the continuance of the bad object. However, seen from the perspective of society-as-a-whole we can begin to understand what religion represents for Islamic society and the way that this is a response to the effects of Globalization. Islamic religion provides Muslim societies with an identity at a time of severe threat to individual and group identity. It is the one constant and enduring institution that provides any form of containment. Seen in this way we can appreciate that the Islamic resurgence is mainstream not extremist, pervasive not isolated. The underlying problem for the West is not Islamic fundamentalism, it is Islam a different culture whose people are proud of its culture but are experiencing severe threats to their culture and their identity as a result of Western Globalization. The West is regarded as a culture whose people is convinced of the universality of their culture and believes that their superior power imposes on them the ability and right to extend that culture throughout the world. These are basic ingredients that fuel the conflict between Islam and the West.

It seems clear that for some while now, members of Muslim societies have felt strongly about the influence and effect of Globalization on their way of life. However, they have been faced with the problem of not being able to counter this threat. From a Muslim perspective the West is seen as being so powerful and mighty an adversary that it seems a near helpless task to stop the progress of Western influence. But that does not mean they will not try. As was the case with regard to the Industrial Revolution, history has shown that no matter what the circumstances may be Muslims have always been brave and stout defenders of their culture. We can be sure that if, as is currently happening, one culture sees another culture increasing its power and thereby becoming a potential threat, it will attempt to protect its own security by strengthening its power and perhaps allying itself with other cultures. A reverse example is that referred to above whereby the West has introduced protectionist measures against China which is threatening Western economic security.

At this time, the West has such overwhelming economic and military power that it can set the agenda. It can take a monocular perspective that simply takes into account the needs of the West by introducing protectionist measures without consideration for non-Western producers of goods—and, as in the Industrial Revolution, respond with the threat that if you don't like it we will move the production elsewhere. Seen from the perspective of the non-Western societies their experience can only be one of powerlessness and hopelessness. In most instances they have no influence on the processes and simply have to do what the West wants them to do. Seen in the light of the first Globalization the oppressed have only one choice and that is to rebel. In that instance the rebellion consisted among other things of destruction of machinery by the Tollpuddle Martyrs. In other words they were mobilized to attack the symbol of their helplessness, the machinery that was driving the change.

It may be significant that those destroying machinery in England in the nineteenth century were referred to as "martyrs". In recent years we have experienced other "martyrs", the Muslim suicide bombers. And of course we cannot forget that the most dramatic suicide bombers were those who hijacked and flew the aeroplanes that were then crashed into the twin towers of the World Trade Center in New York on 9/11. Terrorism is historically the weapon of the weak, that is, of those who do not possess conventional military power. And here we have the direct link between Globalization and global Muslim terrorism. The effect of Globalization on societies throughout the world be that in the West or in non-Western societies is destroying cultures in the same way that the Industrial Revolution did. All societies experience feelings of helplessness but how they cope with this differs according to the unique circumstances. For Muslims, one of the responses is terrorism. And we can now see what the terrorists such as Osama Bin Laden and Al Qaeda represent for Muslim society. Nuclear weapons have also been the weapons by which the weak compensate for conventional inferiority. Separately terrorism and nuclear weapons are the weapons of the non-Western weak. If and when they are combined, the non-Western weak will be strong. This is doubtless why Iran is so keen to acquire nuclear weapons. We may also view Iran as doing something on behalf of Muslim societies.

The analyses in this and the preceding chapter serve to show that Globalization is having such a disruptive effect on the societal cultures of the world as to be causing a degree of suffering and anxiety that is experienced as worse than the effects of terrorism. Feelings associated with "death of a way of life" leading to a loss of identity and disintegration is experienced as madness, chaos, and a fear of death. In such circumstances we might expect extreme responses as attempts to preserve identity. In the next chapter I will continue the analyses by trying to shed more light and understanding on these complicated and dangerous dynamics.

CHAPTER SEVEN

Exploring the effects of Globalization on inter-cultural relationships and relatedness

I n this chapter I will provide a concluding analysis that seeks to build on the analyses of Chapters Four and Five by exploring the effect of Globalization on inter-cultural relationships and relatedness. The aim is to provide a deeper explanation of the resulting inter-cultural dynamics that are having such dangerous consequences at this time. In doing so, I do not seek to attach blame to any particular society, culture, group or individual leader. Rather, I take the position that what has happened and what is happening is simply the consequences of the experiences of members of societies throughout the world. What has happened is not seen in a judgemental way and is neither considered as good nor considered as bad. That is not to say that some things might be done in a more beneficial manner in the future. I would suggest that one of the reasons why things have been as they are is because until now members of societies throughout the world have been largely ignorant of the effects of Globalization. The imperceptible nature of change, even the massive change currently taking place, acts to make us blind to the consequences. Exposure of the destructive effects on societal cultures, most noticeably that which results in global Muslim terrorism, will enable us to think about global dynamics in a different way, which is the aim of this chapter.

The role of individuals

One of the greatest difficulties in developing understanding of this incredible period in the history of the world is that "we" are all part of it. And that no matter what society we are members of, we are part of that societal culture and it is happening to "us". This makes it difficult to step back and reflect on what is happening and while we may be aware of the profound nature of change the detail is largely imperceptible. In addition, it is suggested that we are at a point where we have experienced "death of the old way of life" but have not as yet developed an understanding of the resulting "new way of life". We are at the position where the previous understanding is found to be unhelpful and does not provide explanations for what is happening; at this stage, a new understanding is being developed which will eventually permit clarity but this may take some time to reach. At this moment we are developing a new paradigm or as I would call it a "new way of life". Meanwhile, members of societies throughout the world are left with massive uncertainty, feelings of disintegration, helplessness, hopelessness and a loss of or threat to their identities.

When we experience unbearable thoughts and feelings we are inclined to split them off and blame others. But it is not as simple as that because "we" are all part of and involved in whatever happens. For example, when "we" project our feelings of helplessness into politicians and other societal leaders "we" contribute to their actions. Taking a further example, it may help to reflect on the experience of the members of society in the United States of America immediately after the 9/11 attacks. The relatedness of the USA to other nations is doubtless greatly influenced by the only other major attack on their home territory: that of the attack on Pearl Harbor. On that occasion, it quickly brought about a further active involvement in World War Two. Since then, no other nation, not even during the cold war with the Soviet Union, has attacked Americans on their own soil. I have little doubt that it therefore came as a considerable shock and I equally have little doubt that it resulted in massive anger and hatred for the perpetrators which resulted in massive projections of dependency on the President to "do something". I am also sure that this extended beyond American society to members of other Western societies who likewise projected their dependency onto the President.

Seen from this perspective all Americans, and others in other Western societies, must share responsibility for subsequent actions that include the invasion of Iraq. Had the overt and unconscious dependency not resulted in projections on the President for some sort of revenge a different course of action may have been decided upon. I guess that some might say, "but I didn't do anything". That may be so, but the act of not doing anything means that it enabled the projections of those seeking revenge to dominate. Thus all by being dependent and not taking their own authority must share responsibility for actions. Such are the dynamic processes, which are frequently unconscious, that it is difficult enough to understand our own and other Western experiences let alone that of non-Western societies. But it seems helpful to take our own experiences of Globalization as a starting point.

Democracy as idealized object

In the West, that is, in Western societies, democracy and democratic processes are promoted as some sort of essential component of modern living. Democracy is seen as so all-important that it has become an idealized good object that is not open to challenge and debate. "It" (democracy) is seen as a perfect and wonderful system that is also seen as beyond question. If and when it does become the subject of anything approaching critical debate, the arguments are frequently dismissed by citing the alternatives, and this is put forward as a total and unquestionable defence. In reality, of course, democracy like any other social and political process frequently requires negotiation at the edges.

For example, recent events following the Muslim terrorist attacks on 9/11 have caused considerable furore regarding the way that prisoners are dealt with and evidence obtained at off-shore locations such as Guantanamo Bay where all "normal" rights bestowed on citizens in a democracy such as the basic right to legal advice and appearance before a court have been ignored in the name of defending a democratic way of life. A further example is that concerning the democratic right of free speech, which following the publication by a newspaper in Denmark of a cartoon regarded by Muslims as offensive to Islam, resulted in rioting and attacks on Western diplomatic premises in Muslim countries and demonstrations in many European countries. In the past the maxim "I totally disagree with what you say but support your right to say it" was the norm as part of the democratic process. However, now many were saying that freedom of speech was only acceptable if it did not seriously offend others.

Be it a family, business or international diplomacy that we are referring to, in any relationship both parties will be involved in a system of political relationships and relatedness. They are each connected by their own pool of internal knowledge of roles in other political systems. Doubtless, the West has been influenced by nearly a century of conflicts; first with Dictatorships in Germany and elsewhere; and subsequently, with a Soviet Union Communist backed approach whereby Iron Curtain societies were subjected to a totalitarian process. Compared with both of these alternative forms of social and political life democracy was perhaps understandably idealized. However, this now presents a problem because based on this idealized, unquestioned process "we" in the West have developed a belief that non-Western societies should also commit themselves to the Western values of democracy, including free markets, limited government, human rights, individualism, and the rule of law; and that they should embody these values in their societal institutions.

Islam as idealized object

In the Muslim World, that is, in Muslim societies, Islam and Islamic processes are also promoted as some sort of essential component of modern living. Islam is seen as so all-important that it has become an idealized good object that is also seen as not being open to challenge. "It" (Islam) is seen as a perfect and wonderful system that is beyond question. If and when it does become the subject of anything approaching critical debate the arguments are regarded as sacrilegious and this view is put forward as a total and unquestionable defence. In reality, of course, Islam like any other social and political process frequently requires negotiation at the edges.

For example, one of the effects of Globalization has been the movement of Muslim people to many Western countries. Taking up a role in Western societies has presented considerable problems. These are frequently played out through the young as in France where headscarves and other religious clothing and ornaments are banned from schools. And in England where certain Islamic dress is banned in schools. In the West there are many relaxed attitudes to nudity and other liberal social practices that are not acceptable to Muslims which creates further problems, while women's rights, achieved after a long hard struggle in Western societies are seen as contrary to Islamic belief. These and other problems that challenge their belief system require negotiation and understanding.

Because Islam is not a national culture and lacks a core state, its relations with the West can vary greatly depending on which particular country we are referring to. We should not really be surprised that Muslims fear and resent Western power and the threat which this poses to their society and beliefs. Given that the first Globalization was led by the British and other Western societies, and that this Globalization is led by the American and other Western societies, it seems likely that the fears of Muslim societies are likely to be even greater. They see Western culture as materialistic, corrupt, decadent, and immoral. They also see it as seductive, and hence stress all the more the need to resist its impact on their way of life. Increasingly Muslims attack the West for adhering to an imperfect, erroneous religion.

Doubtless the Islamic world has also been influenced by many centuries of experience that effects their current thinking: from the Crusades, through the Industrial Revolution and colonialization there are many factors that may affect their relatedness to the West. In both societies, Western and Muslim, the singular, monocular view that I referred to in the Preface means that the boundary or interface between the two cultures is seen as an abrasive interface and one that can easily lead to it becoming a battleground. On the surface we all like to believe that "our" society, be that America, Britain, Sweden, or any other Western society, is a wonderful place to live and that this is by far and away the best way of living. In doing so, there is a danger that we may fail to recognize that other ways of living not only exist but are equally regarded by their citizens as wonderful places to live and that they may also be regarded by them as the best way of living. That is most certainly the case with both Islam and China which both embody great cultural traditions very different from and in their eyes infinitely superior to that of the West. It is a seductive thought for members of all societies to consider themselves "the best" but a danger is that they may also view the world from a monocular perspective. In both Islamic and Western societies we are constantly in grave danger of splitting and developing "the other" which is seen as not like us and not such a good place to be.

By virtue of their characteristic sameness and continuity, societal cultures normally provide containment for members of societies and this enables a reflective capacity to exist. In most developed societies we have learned to control our most primitive feelings of hatred and aggression. And in these environmental conditions members of societies can for the most part exist in a mental position where they can see both good and bad in the same people, even though they may be different. However, when the dynamic processes that are also part of our societal cultures dominate, as they do at this time, there is a lack of containment. In these circumstances, as has been detailed above, members of societies feel hopeless, experience fragmentation and disintegration and a subsequent loss of or threat to their identity. This is experienced as chaos and a near death experience where anxiety is immense. At this point members of societies are liable to use primitive defence mechanisms to help them cope. Primary among these processes is splitting whereby we may see ourselves as totally good and others as totally bad.

When we get into this primitive process we tend to idealize, to an excessive degree, our own society, our values and our religion. This excessive idealization is a good indicator that we are engaged in a process of splitting. It is an attempt to protect the good object from aggression by isolating it. At one level this is a very attractive process as the idealization of ones culture can result in feelings of love and commitment to that culture. However, what cannot be ignored is that this moral goodness only exists as a result of splitting off all aggression onto others. In this state we only maintain our idealized feelings at the expense of acts of hatred and aggression against others who we regard as evil. A danger is that the idealization of the beliefs on which societal culture is based becomes so extreme that any possibility of reinterpretation or revision becomes impossible. Any attempt to explore the values, beliefs and religion that are characteristic of our culture is seen as a sort of treason. I referred above to idealization of "democracy" by the West and idealization of "Islam" by Muslims. The descriptions used there are strong indicators of splitting. A result of which is that both Muslims and the West are adding to their differences by each believing and acting on their stereotypes of the other.

"Us" and "them"

The term "culture" is used to refer to the overall way of life of a people. It involves the values, norms, institutions, and modes of thinking to which successive generations in a given society have attached primary importance. In the West "culture" and "cultured" are frequently linked and being cultured is regarded as being civilized. The idea of being civilized was developed by French thinkers at the time of the Industrial Revolution as the opposite of the concept of "barbarism". Civilized society differed from primitive society because it was settled, urban, and literate. To be civilized was good and to be uncivilized was bad. Or indeed, as was previously referred to at the time of the Industrial Revolution, if you didn't wear trousers you were a Barbarian! The tendency to think in terms of two worlds has recurred throughout history. It is classic use of the primitive defence mechanism that we refer to as "splitting". People are always tempted to divide groups and cultures into us and them, the in-group and the other, our culture and those Barbarians. The cultures to which Western and Muslim societies belong are the largest groups with which we strongly identify. Cultures are the biggest "we" within which we feel at home, as distinguished from all the other "thems" out there and our identity depends entirely where or how we draw that boundary line.

We come to feel that "I am this and not that" by drawing a boundary line between "this" and "that" and then recognizing our identity with "this" and our non-identity with "that". For example, we may have a very clear religious conviction and will draw a distinct boundary between ourselves and those who are seen to have different religious convictions. In this way we develop a notion of "me", and everything I psychologically consider to be "me" is on the inside of the boundary. Anything I consider to be "not me" is outside the boundary. In this way we create a psychological boundary between "me" and "not me". An effect is that we now assess "not me's" by their personal beliefs and actions. In this way we make judgements about others as to their inclusion or exclusion. For example we may consider that those who are from our religious conviction will be included in our boundary but others from different religions are outside our boundary. Thus, if I am a Christian then Muslims may be excluded and vice versa.

Psychological boundaries are an important aspect of groups and cultures. In much the same way as we define the boundaries of the individual so do psychological boundaries also define who belongs to a particular group or society and who does not: we move from the me and not me to the "us" and "them". This helps us to understand how the group members distinguish external boundaries, separating members from non-members, and internal boundaries where the phenomenon of scapegoating is frequently observed. This acceptance or rejection of group members is related to the development of inner psychological boundaries. This creates the circumstances whereby immigrants may be physically accepted into a society but at a psychological level they may be regarded as "them" and excluded from the society. This is the experience in many societies throughout the world at this time.

The cultural interface

Identification of and appreciation of boundaries is helpful because we make meaning out of our experiences, and experience itself is at the boundary between the two worlds—external interaction and internal interpretation. The contact point, at the boundary, is where awareness arises. However, as we might suspect, awareness may not be a straightforward experience. Frequently there may not be a match between our internalized knowledge and the external experience. In these circumstances, the ambiguity which exists at the boundary between our personal knowledge and that which is being sensed can be a source of anxiety, and then it is the boundaries that matter. When we experience conflict between inner and outer worlds we tend to concentrate our behaviour on the differences not the similarities. A result is that this makes us feel that the markers of such boundaries are of special value, or sacred or taboo. Contact is the point where the boundaries of the group or society ("us") meet other boundaries, such as those of other social systems ("not us"). The boundary is at the location of a relationship where the relationship both separates and connects.

The development of psychological boundaries provides us with a degree of comfort and wellbeing. But when we perceive our boundaries to be under threat we feel the need for self-preservation. It is as if there is a threat to our very existence and in these circumstances the interface between me and not me may be an abrasive experience. A problem with boundaries is that they can become fixed structural conceptions that prevent learning, as is clearly the situation in regard to the boundary that currently exists between the West and Islam. The contact boundary is where one differentiates oneself from others. If we are familiar with the information being perceived it will be matched with our previous knowledge and dealt with according to whether we like it or dislike it. But a problem arises when we experience new input about which we have no previous knowledge: something that we have never experienced before. In this situation, we need to find a means of coping with the problem presented. One way of dealing with this information is to try to understand the unfamiliar, by accepting the unpleasurable situation and working at it. Another way to deal with the unfamiliar is to link it to some previous category that we think it fits into. While yet another approach is to deny its existence and to filter it out. It will be appreciated that in taking either of the last two options we shall either make a very poor and inappropriate decision or a non-decision.

The current experiences for both members of Muslim societies and members of Western societies is that both are coming to terms with having to face up to new information that we have not previously experienced. Because of our mutual current emotional experiences arising from recent history it seems that few are trying to understand the unfamiliar. Most responses are in the nature of linking the information to some previous category that we think it fits into. For example it seems that at the time of 9/11 many members of Western societies likened what happened to an "act of war" and in doing so they created a conceptual flow of thought that was appropriate to an act of war. It also seems likely that this thought was carried through to the War in Iraq and the War on Terror. The reality of the 9/11 attack was something very different: it was a terrorist act by a group of Muslims who were mobilized by a Muslim society that was experiencing death of a way of life. This level of understanding is only possible if we can try to comprehend the unfamiliar by accepting the unpleasurable situation we are in, and working at a new understanding.

Polarization and splitting

Many features of Western culture contribute to a sense of individualism and a tradition of individual rights and liberties that are unique among societies. Whether these rights are matched with equal notions of responsibilities is perhaps questionable at this time and this may contribute to the view that the dominance of individualism in the West compared to the prevalence of collectivism elsewhere and the values that are most important to the West are least important to members of non-Western societies. There are many issues that create fears for both cultures. For example, Pipes (2002) informs us that Muslims number nearly one billion individuals. They constitute more than 85 per cent of the population in some thirty-two countries; they make up between 25 and 85 percent of the population in eleven other countries; and significant numbers but less than 25 percent in another forty-seven countries. This is in direct contrast to Western societies who are not able to maintain their present numbers. These demographic facts underlie and fuel Western fears of both Muslim culture and of immigration. Population growth permeates the Muslim consciousness with confidence about the future and imbues Westerners with a sense of foreboding.

In the West there is an assumption that increased interaction between people is generating a common world culture. However, the non-Westerners see as Western what the West sees as universal. What Westerners herald as benign global integration, such as the proliferation of worldwide media, is denounced by non-Westerners as nefarious Western imperialism. To the extent that non-Westerners see the world as one, they see it as a threat. As I have previously stated only naive arrogance can lead Westerners to assume that non-Westerners will become "Westernized" by acquiring Western goods. It is a huge mistake to think that blue jeans, cola and popular music can result in a change of societal culture. And, there is little or no evidence that the emergence of pervasive global communications is producing significant convergence in attitudes and beliefs. On the contrary, the evidence would point to attempts to retain and strengthen the existing societal cultures and this results in nationalism. Except of course with regard to Islam which is not nation-bound and thus the support is for the common denominator—Islamic religion.

Difference is at the heart of the difficulties of inter-cultural understanding. As human beings we are preoccupied with difference, going back to that early experience of being separated from mother and with it the splitting and projection that results in mother being experienced as "good" or "bad" but never both good and bad. This continues through our lives and we are ever in danger of splitting and seeing the other as totally bad. This position is enhanced by the fact that we have a strong proclivity to turn difference into polarization. From our earliest experiences we learn that there is no me without an other. But more than that, there is no "me" without the existence of a "not me" that has good or bad values attached to "not me". And if I wish to feel good about myself on any dimension the "not me" has to be seen as bad. For example, when we experience murderous feelings after viewing the horrors of 9/11 or other terrorist outrage, we find these feelings unbearable. We do not want to accept that we could be like that. Those sorts of feelings only belong to "them". And thus we split them off and locate them in the terrorists. Westerners wish to see themselves as cultured, and proud defenders of freedom and democracy. They may regard the "me" as they see it as benevolent, kindly, freedom loving and peaceful. In order to support this view the "not me" are Muslims who are seen as murderous uncivilized Barbarians that distinguish "me" the Westerner as being good.

We need to remind ourselves that there can be no sameness unless there is also a difference. No inclusion without exclusion and we make free use of that word "we" that can in different contexts be interpreted as including or as excluding. It's sometimes uncomfortable to recognize that I am "not me" for the "other". And this sometimes leads to the basic differences that exist between Muslim culture and Western culture being experienced as entirely opposite perceptions of the same experience. A frequent complaint by Muslims is that "Americans come here and want us to be like them. They have no knowledge of our culture history and value." Americans see their actions as benevolent and as being helpful while Muslims see it as attempts to subordinate, humiliate, and undermine Islamic institutions and culture. As Muslims they wish to be seen as independent, religious and proud defenders of an ancient and known way of life. They may regard the "me" as they see it as being devout, kindly people who are content to lead a simple life. However, in order to support this view they need to compare themselves with the "not me". The "not me" are the Westerners who are seen as possessing all the bad Satanic qualities that distinguish "me" the Muslim, as being good.

Displacement and scapegoating

From the analyses of Western and non-Western societies in the last two chapters we may reasonably conclude that the environment that members of all societies are faced with is fragmented and rapidly changing. The effect of the dynamics on societies is such that the required continuity, consistency and confirmation of our world that was first referred to by Kernberg (1966), is absent to a considerable degree. If the possessions and roles by which we gain our continuity, consistency and confirmation are shared in our culture, then we can assume that if we lose our ability to predict and to act appropriately, our world will begin to crumble, and since our view of our self is inextricably mixed up with our view of the world, that too will begin to crumble. If we have relied upon other people or possessions to predict and act in many ways as an extension of our self then the loss of those people or possessions can be expected to have the same effect upon our view of our self as if we had lost a part of our self. A result is that we experience a loss of or threat to our identity. In non-Western societies this engenders aggression and when it cannot be discharged against the frustrating object that is typically the USA, Bush, or Blair it is redirected and displaced toward substitutes such as terrorist targets.

In this context it is interesting to consider the symbolic relevance of the World Trade Center as the target for an attack on Globalization. The experience of Muslim societies is likely to be the same as that of Western societies—awareness that something profound is happening to their world but what precisely is occurring is imperceptible. However, at a subconscious or unconscious level it is probably experienced as an American led, Western attempt through Globalization to control the world through trade. If that is the case, it makes sense that the aggression against Globalization should be redirected and displaced onto the symbol of world trade. The same sort of thing occurs in Western societies where aggression which cannot be discharged against the frustrating object—which is typically Muslims, Islam or Al Quaeda—is displaced toward substitutes such as immigrants. The phenomenon of scapegoat formation is a manifestation of the displacement of aggressive impulses upon an individual or a group. It occurs most often when the expression of these impulses against the substitute object seems less fraught with imagined or real danger than their direct expression. I previously referred to the responsibility of all members of society for actions taken by their leaders. One of the reasons that we support our leaders is because of the felt insecurity. However dissatisfied we may be with them we need to protect them and it is safer to put our negative projections into Muslims or whoever. Where the environment is not experienced as a safe place members of societies are inclined to resort to less mature, primitive behaviour.

Leadership and societal projection

At this point I want to briefly return to the earlier discussion regarding projection onto the President or other societal leaders. This is the process of attributing one's own unacceptable thoughts and feelings to others. It is the thrusting forth onto the external world, or perhaps more accurately into another person or group, of an individual's unconscious wishes and ideas that would be painful if accepted as part of the self. Thus, when members of societies feel helpless, hopeless and disoriented they become dependent and split off these thoughts and feelings and project them into political and other societal leaders who they are encouraging to do something. A result of this projection of unwanted thoughts and feelings may result in members of societies being left in a position where they may now blame "them", the political or other leaders, for their failures. In effect, we will have all contributed to the actions of "them". And when we in our despair project all our unwanted thoughts and feelings into our leaders we are as responsible for their actions as they are.

Faced with the aggressive projections of their societies "to do something" and to rescue "us" from our dependence and helplessness it may be no surprise that political leaders feel the need to "do something". We might hope that our leaders, whether Western or non-Western, will have the wisdom and ability to understand that members of societies are facing chaos and loss of or threats to their identity and are therefore likely to be frightened, even to the extent that they are seeking a Messianic figure to save them. And that this is being done for the not least purpose of saving them from their own feelings of hatred and aggression. With such wisdom, political leaders may be able to provide the containment necessary for members of societies to feel hope and security. Such leaders will not exaggerate the goodness of their own culture and the badness of the other. The understanding leader who is able to take a reflective stance and view things in a way that will not protect his own leadership or the unity of his or her society by demonizing others serves a vital function on behalf of society. This requires leadership that is based on an ability to interpret the traditional values of the society in such a way that it includes the "other", without utterly reconstructing the "other" and denying their true "otherness".

That is not to deny the difficulty of societal leaders for withstanding the desire by the members of society to mobilize them in this primitive manner. Our leaders are, at the end of the day, human, the same as other members of society, and being human are subject to all the same primitive processes as the rest of us. I feel sure that at times they may also be feeling helpless, and experiencing fragmentation and disintegration and a subsequent loss of or threat to their identity. And, as it is for each of us, this is experienced by them as chaos and a near death experience in which anxiety is immense. It is likely therefore that at this point, without a reflective capacity, societal leaders also use primitive defence mechanisms to help them cope. Not least the process of splitting whereby they and we see ourselves as totally good, and others as totally bad. This would appear to be the case with regard to both Western and Muslim leaders. This is shown in the discussion on the use of "democracy" and "Islam" which provides us with a strong indication that the primitive process of splitting is occurring in both societies. In addition, we can see in the statements of both Western and Muslim leaders strong indicators that the "other" is being denigrated, and demonized to the extent that they are wholly bad. Typical are the statements by Western leaders about the "axis of evil", and "the global terror network"; and by Muslims about "the great infidel".

Society-as-a-whole

Throughout the book I have followed a stance that views societies from a group-as-a-whole perspective. This systemic process may be unusual to many readers and may run contrary to other more individualistic approaches. However, those who take a more traditional approach appear to find that this presents difficult questions. For example, Pipes (2002) asked some fairly basic questions. "What is the connection between Islam and the acts of violence carried out in its name?" "Is it useful to distinguish between Islam and the extreme version of the religion known variously as militant Islam, radical Islam, fundamentalist Islam, or Islamism?" "Is it further useful to distinguish between the violent and the political variants of militant Islam?" "Can Al Qaeda be ascribed to a cult rather than to Islam?" "Does militant Islam result from poverty?" and, "Are Islamists medieval?" He also asked, "With whom or what is the United States at war?" Pipes most helpfully states that, "the answer to this question has far-reaching implications for strategy, for public diplomacy, and for foreign and domestic policy alike".

As has been stated in Chapter Four above, the answer to most of these questions and in regard to the strategy for public diplomacy, and for foreign and domestic policy determined and followed by most Western governments in their dealing with Muslim societies, is that stated by President Clinton, President Bush and Prime Minister Blair who have argued that the West does not have problems with Islam but only with violent Islamic extremists. This is a sort of displacement whereby the hatred and aggression for Muslims is split off and projected into parts of Islam such as Al Qaeda as a means of avoiding the reality that they are in disagreement with the members of all Muslim societies. To consider such a possibility may be much too scary and it is easier to displace the anger onto a small part of Islam such as Al Qaeda. It is a world in which leaders are heightening anxieties by, for example, producing threat assessments on the one hand and on the other hand denying real danger, for example by ignoring jihads on writers. For those concerned, such denials may leave them feeling that they face a more manageable problem but this is a no less dangerous position than to designate the whole of the Muslim world as evil.

Not least, it is a denial of reality and an omnipotent phantasy that political and societal leaders can control and protect members of societies from the aggression and hatred of the other. It is also a denial of the notion of viewing a society as a society, or to put it another way, a denial of the existence of societal culture. By way of a reminder, the field of study whereby we view society as a whole is one where role is defined as a property of the society, and role prescriptions are filled, sometimes by individuals, sometimes by sub-groups and sometimes by identifiable clusters of behaviour that are a societal property and serve a role function. These group or societal role dynamics are to be seen as a manifestation of the group or society-as-a-whole. Thus, for example, Al Qaeda is to be seen as a sub-group of Islam that is doing something on behalf of Muslim society-as-a-whole.

If we have any doubts about this approach I would invite you to recall the cheering and excited crowds who gathered in many Muslim countries as televisions around the world carried pictures of the twin towers crashing to the ground. There is also some evidence to support the notion that members of Muslim societies had been informed in advance that something important was about to happen—on their behalf. Viewing societal dynamics in this way we can better answer the questions posed by Pipes. Seen from the perspective of society-as-a-society we can understand that there is a connection between Islam and Al Qaeda and other fundamentalist and terrorist organizations and actions. The actions of Al Qaeda and other terrorist groups and of nations such as Iran are to be seen as manifestations of Muslim societies. They are being mobilized to do something on behalf of Muslim societies everywhere. Demonizing and killing those mobilized to commit acts of terror may be necessary but it will not serve to provide a solution which lies in developing a relationship with the whole Muslim society.

Standing back from the current problem it may be helpful to explore a further terrorist example. By taking a systemic view of the activities of the Irish Republican Army (IRA) it enables us to see the situation in a different light. Seen from the perspective that the IRA are simply terrorists and criminals who carry out evil atrocities in an inhuman manner that is a sort of punishment or revenge for past activities is a view frequently put forward. However, when we take a systemic view and see the IRA as doing something on behalf of the whole Irish society we get a very different understanding. There is frequent comment about whether such groups are terrorists or freedom fighters. This is not helpful because it simply involves splitting, depending on whichever view you may be taking. Seen from a systemic perspective, we can see them as part of a wider problem, as part of the total Irish system, a small sub-group who are being mobilized by the total system to do something on their behalf. As with the cheering crowds in Muslim countries after the horrors of 9/11, so also was there widespread support for the IRA throughout Irish society, including those who had emigrated to the USA, and elsewhere.

In effect, this is no different to what is happening in Western societies. So, before going any further I want us to consider that what is happening in the West is not happening without our complicity. To a greater or lesser degree we are colluding with Western governments in this process. We may seek to "blame" Bush or Blair or the USA but we are all part of this process. We projected our anxiety into our leaders when we were faced with the anguish and pain of the stockmarket crash and of continuing worrying economic trends and we are all benefiting from the results of Globalization. In like manner, we all projected our helplessness and dependence into Bush, Blair and other Western leaders when the terrorists struck and we all asked them "to do something" on our behalf. I make no judgement about whether what "they" did was right or wrong, rather it is what happened as a result of the dynamics that were occurring at that time. The key thing is for all members of societies to accept their part in these (continuing) dynamics and stop blaming "them". When members of societies take their own authority for their actions we can expect a more mature debate and a more realistic approach to the problems we face.

If members of society ("us") continue to act like sheep they must accept the consequences. If for example, we unconsciously provide support to the way that political leaders idealize our way of life, then we must accept the consequences as must members of Muslim societies accept the consequences if they behave in a similar way with regard to their leaders. The bombings in London brought a response from the British Prime Minister that was taken up by others that "they" (the bombers) "will not destroy our way of life". No one seemed capable of considering the fact that this was the very reason that Muslims were giving for their terrorist attacks. The London suicide bomber Mohammed Sadique Khan in a prepared statement before his death stated: "Your democratically elected governments continuously perpetuate atrocities against my people all over the world. . . . Until we feel security, you will be our targets. And until you stop the bombing, gassing, imprisonment and torture of my people we will not stop this fight." They (Muslims) were also concerned with preserving their way of life. They, just like members of Western societies are concerned with "the death of a way of life" as an effect of Globalization. In like manner, the President of the USA talks of "bringing democracy to the middle east" in such a way that this is a good thing that will result in advances in their way of living. It seems that the view is one which says that what's good for us must be good for them. Instead of resisting the aggressive projections of members of societies Western and Muslim leaders are acting on them. All this does is to encourage splitting and further projection by members of societies.

Following Pipes, and having regard for the far-reaching implications for strategy, for public diplomacy, and for foreign and domestic policy, I would suggest that there is a considerable need for "psychologically informed politicians". If they were so informed they might have a better understanding of current inter-societal or inter-cultural dynamics and of our own societal dynamics. The statements of both Western and Muslim leaders that denigrate, and demonize the "other" leads us to conclude that both are engaged in primitive processes. Behaving in this way can only result in members of societies acting in the same manner. It becomes a collusive process that in turn becomes part of Western and Muslim culture. A result is a sort of institutionalized hatred of Muslims and vice versa.

The danger is that idealization of one's own society results in a total disregard for other societies. Such is the nature of this splitting process that those concerned are unable to begin to consider that the "other" can be both good and bad even though they may be different. Western leaders, and members of Western societies, cannot begin to think that Muslims can be both good and bad at the same time. And of course, the same applies to Muslim leaders and members of Muslim societies who cannot begin to consider that Westerners can be both good and bad. A result of this way of thinking and behaving is that we act "as if" the other party does not exist, that they are inhuman and not therefore subject to our usual way that we think and feel about our fellow human beings. The danger is that when our politicians engage in such behaviour it can only lead to us all acting in the same way, that is, to ignore what is happening with regard to the other party to the relationship.

Emotions and stereotyping

At times there may be good reason why we find it so very hard to consider the "other". An effect of terrorism is that the atrocities are such that our emotions are aroused to such a degree that we are unable to reflect. Viewing the terrible and highly distressing effects of 9/11 or the London Underground bombings we may be so overwhelmed by our emotions that we are not able to listen and not able to think. We are flooded with murderous, and perhaps racist feelings and thoughts; and of desires for revenge to the degree that we cannot cope. We are so emotionally incapacitated that we are unable to reflect and think clearly. We are scared by the very thoughts and feelings that we are experiencing. We deal with them by splitting off all evil thoughts and feelings and locating them in the bombers who are then demonized. And if we are not careful we then stereotype all Muslims and treat them as demons or Barbarians. Stereotyping is a form of defensive behaviour that we use to deny difference, and may be defined as fixed, inflexible notions about an individual or group, and are at the heart of prejudice. They block our ability to think about individuals or groups as the "other" (the outsider) and concentrate on the "differences" between "us" and "them".

This, I felt, was remarkably well understood by members of a Listening Post in Birmingham, England in July 2005 which it will be appreciated was held shortly after the London bombings. There were two hypotheses resulting from the analysis. The first hypothesis, "The 'them' in 'us': denial of hateful feelings", stated:

> Faced with an awareness of highly emotional murderous events and threats to their personal safety members of society split off all hateful feelings and locate them in the bombers and those suspected of being bombers. The result is that fixed, inflexible notions about individual bombers or groups identified as associated with bombers are developed which results in demonization of these individuals and groups. The associated emotion, in turn, blocks the ability of members of society to think about these individuals and groups or even to listen to views that are contrary to those they hold. Hatred and revenge then become the natural responses and understanding becomes a near impossibility.

The second hypothesis, "The have's and have not's: the shadow over my neighbour", stated:

> Our fear of the other and the threat to our identity have been awakened by the bombings. Members of society are struggling to come to terms with the basic conflicts surrounding the issue of preservation of "our" way of life as opposed to the effect that this is having on other people's way of life. Having a common enemy in the Muslim bombers helps us to suppress our guilt and to assert our right to the preservation of our way of life. Yet in a strange way this understanding of self can also lead to an understanding of the bombers who may also be seen as asserting *their* right to the preservation of *their* way of life. [Stapley 2005a]

A London Listening Post at New Year of 2005 also referred to this process in a more general way as under:

> Rage associated with helplessness is projected into "the other". There is currently a profound sense of uncertainty in society about socially acceptable behaviour, norms and values. The boundaries of decency are blurred, and there is no consensus about what is permissible and what is not. As a result we are filled with rage and hurt which we project into marginalized groups we then perceive as "barbarians" who carry the blame for social erosion. However this process leaves us depleted and uncertain how to act. [Stapley 2005b]

I can imagine that some readers may take the view that those who engage in terrorist activities such as 9/11 must be evil people. There can be no doubt that they all carried out an evil act. However, I would suggest that one of the surprising things that others have commented on is the "ordinariness" of the 9/11 hijackers. Before this dreadful event they would have been mostly seen as non-violent individuals who offended no one. Indeed, that was probably one of the reasons why they were able to proceed without raising suspicion. What seems certain is that those involved in the 9/11 attack had a proclivity to act in support of their known way of life and as such were easily mobilized to participate. Others, such as Osama Bin Laden and Abu Musab al-Zarqawi in Iraq, may have a proclivity to be aggressive or violent and as such are easily mobilized to act in that way on behalf of Islamic society. But even though it be the case that there may be several people involved in carrying out terrorist acts having been mobilized to act on behalf of Muslim society, we should remember that these individuals were not mobilized to act in this way until recent years. In this respect the comparative data in Chapter Two, which shows the parallel development of Globalization and Al Qaeda, is a helpful reminder. It was only when Globalization started to have an effect on societies throughout the world that the global Muslim terrorist groups were mobilized to carry out their gruesome work.

Given the undeniable evidence, that Muslims see Western culture as materialistic, corrupt, decadent, and immoral and one which adheres to an imperfect, erroneous religion we should not be surprised if their experience was precisely the same as ours. And at times there may be good reason why they also find it so very hard to consider the "other". Coming on top of what is perceived as an attempt to re-impose imperial control through the medium of Globalization they are already suffering extreme anxiety. Added to this, when they view the terrible and highly distressing effects of the Iraq war, of the abuse of prisoners in Abu Graib prison, and the treatment of prisoners around the world, we may reflect that Muslims may also be so overwhelmed by their emotions that they are not able to listen and not able to think. They too, are flooded with murderous, and perhaps racist feelings and thoughts; and of desires for revenge to the degree that they cannot cope. They are so emotionally incapacitated that they are unable to reflect and think clearly. They are scared by the very thoughts and feelings that they are experiencing. And they deal with them by splitting off all evil thoughts and feelings and locating them in the West who are then demonized. And if they are not careful they then stereotype all Westerners and treat them as demons or Satanic.

Inter-cultural relations

Globalization has brought us to a point where inter-societal or inter-cultural relationships are at a dangerous level of misunderstanding and conflict. Viewing terrorism and terrorists as representing something on behalf of Islam as opposed to some criminal fundamentalist sect or Barbarians can change our perception and lead to greater understanding. In the West there are frequent protests and demonstrations against the symbolic leaders of Globalization. In the main these are protests against American-based multinational companies such as Microsoft and McDonalds or the large scale protests at meetings where world leaders are in attendance, such as G8 meetings. These protest groups are being mobilized by and are representing Western societies discomfort with Globalization. As such they are seldom acting from their own authority as opposed to acting on behalf of society. In other cultures the effects of Globalization are almost certainly felt more strongly and the results are also much stronger. Terrorism is seen as a direct response to Western influence and "death of the way of life". The terrorists are to be seen as being mobilized by that society and representing their anger.

Understanding relationships seems a vital development if we are to make progress. In any relationship both parties will be involved in a system of political relationships and relatedness. They are each connected by their own internal knowledge of roles in other political systems. In this instance the level of political system within which the parties may perceive themselves to be related is as a set of inter-cultural relationships. For example, any relationship between West-erners and Muslims will very likely be affected by the baggage which each carries as a result of international relationships developed over previous centuries. Crusaders and non-believers immediately come to mind, as will the derivation of Christian and Muslim religions. In like manner, relationships between Americans and Chinese will likely be affected by different life styles and cul-tures. The political system at the international level will be shaped by history and by national cultures and politics, and these are bound to have some effect on individual or group relationships in which they are involved.

Faced with a situation where many Westerners stereotypically view Muslims as uneducated peasants who treat women as virtual slaves, and live their lives subjected to tyrannical fundamentalist reli-gious leaders; while at the same time Muslims are stereotypically viewing Westerners as corrupt, disbelievers and infidels; that the ways of Christians and Jews "are based on sick or deviant views"; and that "imitating (non-Muslims) leads to a permanent abode in hellfire"; we might conclude, what a recipe for misunderstanding and conflict!

In developing a relationship, there will undoubtedly be ambiguity at the boundary that can be a source of anxiety. Contact is at the point where the boundaries of the society ("us") meet other bound-aries, such as those of another social system ("not us"). In highly difficult circumstances there may be what I shall term a "double boundary". By this I mean a clear boundary around each culture. The sort of circumstance where neither party is intending to budge from their own respective position. The danger is that if we concen-trate our behaviour on the differences not the similarities, this makes the boundaries seem like barriers. Truth is that there are likely to be many, many differences between "us" in the Western world and "them" in the Muslim world. If we are to co-exist in a peaceful and cooperative manner there is a need for both parties to take a binocular view which means having an in-depth understanding of the other.

It is not simply a matter of knowing the "other" better that will result in a more effective relationship. I feel quite certain that most of us would agree with this sort of statement in much the same way that we would agree with the virtues of "apple pie" or "fried rice"; and they are about as useful. Learning about the dynamics of life is a matter that has to be considered in the context of a relationship between two people, or two groups of people, or two cultures. As Gregory Bateson (1979), pointed out, it is correct (and a great improvement) to begin to think of the two people to the interaction as two eyes, *each giving a monocular view* of what goes on and *together giving a binocular view* in depth. This double view is the relationship. Relationship is not internal to the single person or group. Indeed, it would be nonsense to talk about "dependency" or "aggression" or "prejudice" and so on as an individual activity. We cannot be dependent unless there is someone to be dependent on; we cannot be aggressive unless there is someone to be aggressive with; and, we cannot be prejudiced unless there is someone to be prejudiced about. All such words have their roots in what happens between persons (or cultures), not in something-or-other inside a person (or culture).

Entering into a "relationship" means that you do not have to lose your "self" concept and neither does the other individual, group or culture. Indeed, the nature of a relationship is a mutual recognition of sameness and difference that results in the binocular vision described above. However, before we can reach a position where we can see things through both eyes we need to escape from our own monocular vision. If we are so concerned and pre-occupied with our own situation, because, for example, we are suffering from the after shock of a terrorist bombing, we shall be unlikely to be able to get beyond thinking about ourselves. Where that is the case, as has been said, we may respond by using the other individual or group as a means of easing our own distress by, for example, stereotyping or scapegoating. In doing so we accentuate the way we both behave so that we hide behind our individual boundaries taking some comfort that there are others not like us and that we are not like them.

The difficulty is that in accentuating the differences we may also exaggerate them. Thus, for example, Muslims may come to be seen by members of Western societies as demons and Barbarians; while Western people may come to be seen by Muslims as corrupt, decadent and immoral. There is something satisfying, for both sides, in being able to say "I am not like them". By accentuating the difference we can disown parts of ourselves that we don't like. In effect, this is what happens regarding scapegoating. Here, there is a displacement of, say, prejudice onto an individual or a group. It is easier to displace these impulses onto someone who we consider "corrupt" or "immoral" than it is to displace them onto someone we regard as an equal. Thus, when we are faced with personal, group or cultural problems which we cannot handle and which cause us to become increasingly anxious, one of the ways we deal with these feelings, is to look to displace them onto someone else, a culture, group or individual and blame them for what is happening. Thus, it no longer becomes our "failings" but their "failings" which are the cause of the problem. This is something that all human beings do to a greater or lesser extent—if we are not aware of our actions.

Political activity has particular implications for societies involved in relationships. We might consider that every relationship between two societies is a constant psychological negotiation in which each is trying to impose on the other their picture of the other and correspondingly also to ensure that the other's picture of them fits, or is the same as, their picture of them self. That is the politics of identity. When there is a goodness of fit between the two sets of pictures it produces a sense of stability and security. This process is naturally complicated by unrecognized and unconscious wishes that may contradict what we overtly say and believe. It will inevitably depend upon the way each perceives the other and the thoughts and feelings that are evoked about them. And of course many of our formed views may be based on phantasy and emotions.

"Us as we see us" and "us as others see us"

A further difficulty that affects the process of meaning making is that for each party to the relationship there may be two versions of "us". These may be categorized as "us as we see us" and "us as others see us". The "us as we see us" will be determined by our own know-ledge and feelings. The "us as others see us" will be determined by the other's own internalized knowledge and feelings. Suffice to say that these two versions of us may be very different. This will inevit-ably lead to a situation where there are problems of communicating with each other, and that expectations of either or both may not be met or may be working against each other. In which case there may be a breakdown in the relationship, if indeed there is to be any relationship at all.

No matter that our intentions may be positive and that we are truly intent on developing a good relationship with another party that is only "us as we see us". We need to consider that the other party may have a very different view. They may, for example, view us as a society who are going to be difficult to deal with and not interested in developing a good relationship at any price. That is "us as others see us", which for them is an equally real experience. Taking a further example, leaders and members of American society may have a view of the "us as we see us" which is a generous, kindly society that spends billions of dollars to help alleviate poverty and suffering throughout the world; and uses its military power to deliver the oppressed from their plight. This is not unlike the sort of view that was put forward by the British and other European soci-eties when they colonized large parts of the world as a result of the first Globalization. However, the "us as (Muslim) others see Amer-ica" is a very different construct. This view sees America as not being engaged in some benign global integration but as being engaged in some nefarious Western imperialism. In these circum-stances it may be difficult for Americans to understand how such generous actions can be so rudely criticized. At first glance they could be forgiven for feeling hurt and rejected. However, that is to deny the existence of the other reality. When they react in this way this response is likely to be met by the Muslim "other" with a form of "told you so" response.

And of course it also applies the other way round. Leaders and members of Muslim societies have a view of "us as we see us" of themselves as defenders of a way of life that is guided by Islamic law which provides a decent and just way of life. However the "us as seen by (Western) others" is again a very different construct. This view sees Muslims as a non-pluralist society that does not provide rights to women and members of other faiths. These two views of self are ever present. Regardless of our views and our intentions "us as we see us" and "us as others see us" may by very different views of this same "us". As has been demonstrated above a lack of mutual understanding of the considerably different views is resulting in splitting, polarization and stereotyping which are bringing about some ghastly results not least brutal acts of global Muslim Terror.

Taking a systemic view helps us to understand the current situation. At this time, in spite of the considerable clash of cultures and inability to co-exist there cannot be a war between the West and Islam. The West is far too powerful, its military capacity is so great that any war would quickly end in victory for the West. However, that does not mean that war is not possible. Indeed we might recall that Osama Bin Laden declared war on the USA. And in another sense while not a formal declaration there exists a Jihad or war on the West. Wars can be fought in many ways depending on one's capacity. For example in the last World War French resistance fighters carried on a form of war against the invading Germans with whatever capacity they could muster. The guerrilla tactics employed probably had minor consequences to the enemy. However, when viewed from a systemic perspective, the resistance was doing something for and on behalf of French society. It was part of an overall attempt to achieve French independence. They were doing something important on behalf of French society as a whole: they were waging war against the enemy and showing themselves to be not totally helpless.

A systemic approach enables us to understand that terrorism is not an isolated response by a small group of fundamentalists who simply hate the West. Rather it is a Muslim response to the massive effects of Globalization that is resulting in threats to and loss of identity to most if not all societies throughout the world. It has particularly dramatic effects on Islamic societies in view of historical and religious differences. Muslim terrorists, like the French resistance fighters in the last war, and the IRA, are seen to be parts of Muslim society who are mobilized to fight on behalf of the society as a whole. If we are seeking ways forward we need to consider that the views of Al Qaeda may also be the views of all in Muslim societies. This inevitably means not only those in Muslim countries but also those who are immigrants in Western societies.

In this respect, we should not forget the effect of Globalization on Western societies has also been highly disturbing. An experience that is labelled "death of a way of life" and such severe disintegration as to be a threat to the very identity of members of western societies is as bad as it can get. Little surprise, then, that one of the effects has been the impact on different parts of Western societies. For example, in France Muslim youth was mobilized to protest against the way that Muslims in general were being treated. They were living in some of the poorest housing conditions, their work opportunities were either non-existent or only in low paid jobs, they were feeling racially abused, and there was little governmental support for their position. All in all they individually and collectively felt that their identity was threatened. It is a situation not unlike the working classes at the time of the Industrial Revolution, they really had no option but to rebel. A further example is Australia, where the host community have experienced the effect of Globalization as an intrusion to their way of life. A result is that mainly young members of the host community were mobilized to rebel against immigration. Faced with threats to their identity they displaced the anger and frustration onto immigrants who were then "blamed" for all ills.

Some unintended results of Globalization

When politicians and the Media take an approach based on splitting it leads to others also adopting such an approach. Employing splitting may enable us to cope with the hideous experience of terrorism but it results in members of Western societies seeing Muslims as wholly bad and incapable of good. We see them in black and white terms. In this world there is no grey, no possibility of being capable of both good and bad. If because of our own anxiety in dealing with this other of different culture, we project into them our own feelings of anger and other primitive feelings there is every chance that they will become the sort of pariahs that we want them to be. A result is that they may become demonized and considered to be non-human barbaric objects. And, of course, once we have reached the stage of viewing them as non-human Barbarian objects we may now treat them in all manner of ways that are not affected by our conscience.

If this is the view of political leaders, the Media, and members of Western societies we might ask if it is of any wonder that members of Western armed forces should do something on behalf of society given the opportunity. Is it any wonder that soldiers should treat prisoners as inhuman objects as was the case at Abu Graib prison. Is it any wonder that they should kill people including children and old people as is alleged at Haditha. These Acts and those committed by Al Qaeda and other Muslim groups are the sort of results that come about if societal leaders do not take a reflective approach—a collusive sort of Islamophobia or Westernophobia. Idealization of one's own society enables us to disown our own imperfections. When that includes a denial of our capacity for aggressive and murderous thoughts it impoverishes us and leaves us in a child-like state. Where we demonize the "other" and split off and project all our unbearable feelings and thoughts into them we are equally impoverished and again we are left in a child-like state. There is a need for a mature approach whereby societal leaders and members of society do not try to protect themselves or their society by idealizing their own society and demonizing others. Taking a mature stance means that we own our own unbearable thoughts and feelings and accept that we are imperfect and capable of the same sort of behaviour as that we are seeking to blame. It also involves seeing the "other" as they are, and not creating an artificial monster of them.

We might ask why should we, and they, bother? Why should we, and they, try to build a relationship with people who are so different and seemingly committed to destroying our way of life? There is one really good reason why we should work hard at developing real relationships with those of non-Western cultures. In trying to understand what is happening regarding "death of a way of life" we can say that the world is both disintegrating and beginning the process of forming along new lines. At this time, the philosophical assumptions, underlying values, social relations, customs, and overall outlooks on life differ significantly among cultures. And one of the effects of the current changes to our way of life in whatever society we come from is the revitalization of religion, which at this time is reinforcing these differences. The fact that we all, wherever we come from, start with this basic sameness, a severe threat to our identity, means that we immediately share something. And it means that we could work together to develop a new understanding that took account of the need for a pluralist world community.

Increased interaction may not bring about a common culture as was foolishly aimed at by the economists but it does facilitate the transfer of techniques, inventions, and practices from one society to another with a speed and to a degree that were impossible a few decades ago. A sobering thought may be the fact that the processes that we in the West use in Globalization are available to others also. Precisely how others will seek to use this knowledge will vary from society to society. Some will attempt to emulate the West and to join with or bandwagon with the Western multi-national companies. I have in mind the Eastern European countries that were part of the Soviet bloc who are pleased to become part of the European Union and to provide their resources to the benefit of themselves and other richer European nations. Others may choose to develop in their own way using the knowledge obtained from the West to develop their own brand of Globalization. The most obvious example is that of China which is currently building its economic and military capacity at a rate far in excess of the West. Non-Western societies can and have modernized without abandoning their own cultures and adopting wholesale Western values, institutions, and practices. Japanese modernization occurred when a dynamic group of reformers studied and borrowed Western techniques, practices and institutions. They modernized in a way that preserved Japanese culture.

However, that is not the case with regard to Muslim societies. As was explained in Chapter Two, there are several reasons why Muslim culture is considerably different to even Chinese culture. It will be recalled that among the reasons given was the fact that Muslim societies are economically and militarily weak compared with some other non-Western societies. Muslim or Islamic society is part of many nations and does not have a specific national voice to provide a political response. And it is not wealthy enough to provide a copy-cat economic response such as that of the South Americans and Chinese. And, as was concluded, this really leaves them with few options and the response of Muslim or Islamic societies is to aggressively reject Western values and attempts to impose a Western way of life on them. What was not mentioned in the earlier discussion was the dominant influence on Muslim societal culture of Islam. One of the consequences of Globalization is that many Muslims now live in Western societies and as the saying goes, "you can take the Muslim out of Muslim society but you can't take the Muslim society out of the Muslim".

The intercultural interface in Western societies

This raises the important matter of what Muslims bring with them when they become members of Western societies. Essentially what they bring is what all of us bring if we go from one society to another, they and we bring our culture, the way of life that provides for the continuity, consistency and confirmation of our respective worlds. That culture is important to us all is vividly revealed by the many researches that have shown that those moving to a new society frequently experience culture shock that can be a highly emotional and near death experience. We might consider that coming from one society where members of that society were experiencing death of their way of life and a loss of identity, what might be the additional effect of culture shock. These are important matters that need to be understood if we are to develop any sort of relationship. But we also need to understand something more about the nature of the culture that they bring. We need to start by exploring the environment they come from and the sort of "society in the mind" that they are likely to develop. Muslim societal culture unlike most other national societal cultures is near synonymous with Islam. The values, attitudes and beliefs of members of Muslim societies are influenced by this dominant institution, which controls much of the Muslim way of life. It is an environment that does not accept pluralism of religion which virtually means that political, social, and economic policies and processes are also influenced by Islam. Given such a societal holding environment, members of Muslim societies adopt forms of behaviour that they feel are appropriate under the circumstances that they perceive are imposed upon them by their environment. Inevitably this means a society in the mind and behaviour that is dominated by Islam.

I would suggest that this is a culture that is more unitary than even that of the societies living under the totalitarian regimes in the Soviet Union. Being based on a religious rather than a national or political influence it is also more likely that the culture will remain largely unchanged no matter what environment Muslims may be living in. Many immigrants from other societies have become socialized into their new environment. It would seem that this could be a more difficult task for Muslims who are constantly in touch with their culture through Islam. A result is to bring the interface between Western and Muslim cultures into Western societies with some highly dangerous and sometimes violent results. There have been serious confrontations at the boundary between Muslim immigrants and members of Western societies that have left communities puzzled and aghast that such things could happen in what for many years they have considered to be a humane and liberal society. In reality this is no different to the inter-cultural collision at the interface between Western and Muslim culture where the response of Muslim or Islamic societies is to aggressively reject Western values and attempts to impose a Western way of life on them. In the examples that follow it will be seen that this can result in Muslim terrorism and other acts of violence.

A prime example of the sort of struggle that is going on in Western societies is provided in the following extract from a Danish Listening Post Report (part of an OPUS Global Project January 2006):

> "Ambivalence, feelings of guilt, muddled sensations and frustrated energy could be interpreted as a potential for political action directed at defending civic rights for all, for an involvement in real exchange between ethnic groups, for working with what it means both to be a world citizen and a citizen in a nation and a local community."

It will be recalled that shortly after this a Danish journalist was mobilized by Danish society to publish a cartoon of the Prophet Mohammed which was to test the issue of what it means to be a Danish citizen, through the application of their long standing right to free speech. As is also well known, the publication of this cartoon resulted in massive anger among Muslims that may be seen as a measure of their struggles with Globalization. Many Muslims were mobilized on behalf of Muslim societies to protest and display their anger in many Western and non-Western countries.

This example provides us with a graphic picture of the way that a conflict is played out as a microcosm of the effect of Inter-cultural conflict. Taking a society-as-a-whole perspective we can see this conflict as resulting from the way that Globalization impacts on the inter-societal level between the West and Muslim societies. When this conflict is reduced to the national, large group, small group or even individual level, the inter-societal level of relatedness is still part of the experience; it is within the individuals concerned and will thus affect relationships. Danish culture is within the members of Danish society and Muslim culture is within the Muslim members of Danish society. As in the example referred to above, the potential for disaster is ever present and if there is a lack of trust that potential will almost certainly be realized.

A question that is frequently posed about the bombings in London by British Muslim terrorists is "Were they acting on their own?" Behind the question lies some sort of disbelief that British Muslims could possibly hate their fellow Britain's enough to do such an atrocious thing. The members of the host community cannot believe they were acting on their own and want to be able to blame the acts on the influence of Al Qaeda or other Muslim terrorists far away. If they cannot split off these feelings of hatred towards the bombers by seeing them and locating them in part of some "evil empire" they are left with their projections and having to try to understand what part they, the host community, played in these atrocities. Not that it will be any relief to the host community but in a sense the bombers were not acting on their own. We, in Britain, are constantly involved in a system of political relationships and relatedness with members of British society. But it is not only our membership of British society that connects us. That system is competing with and having to mediate, roles in other political systems beyond British society that we perceive as connecting us to a past or future relationship (Miller, 1985). We all have multiple identities and we all view the world through the multiple lenses of those identities. Sometimes those lenses coincide with others and at other times they are in conflict with others.

At a wider level we are all constantly involved in a set of international relationships. Depending on our individual and group experience, we may all have different perceptions based on our constructs of this international system. Thus someone raised and educated in a Muslim country that was now living in Britain might have a totally different perception of current events than someone raised and educated in Britain all their life. On some occasions they may both have the same perception. For example, this may be the case with regard to issues of equal opportunities for all races and availability of schooling for their children. Or in international affairs they may share a view about the evils of communism. However, for some part of the time there is likely to be disagreement and both sides may mobilize feelings, attitudes and stereotypes that derive from their differing roles in society. For example, this is most likely to be the case with regard to such matters as the Iraq war where Muslims are viewing it from their cultural perspective that it is an act of "the great Satan"; and the host community from a Western cultural perspective that sees Iraq as part of an "evil empire".

A recent attempt by the British Government to develop a greater understanding of British values put forward the notion of teaching children the history and development of values as a means of encouraging greater integration of British culture or way of life. When asked about the likely effect this would have on Muslims, a spokesperson said, "It won't work because of the unjust and unfair foreign policy of the Government." Here we can see the effect on Muslims of international relationships developed over a long period of time. The Government views on foreign policy clearly run counter to those of Muslim societies around the world. And it is with Muslim societies that British Muslims identify in regard to the way Britain treats Muslim peoples overseas.

Taking another example, we can view the conflict in Holland that began with the mobilization of the Dutch film maker Theo van Gogh as a leader for the host community and his subsequent murder by Muslims as the micro-politics of the enormous struggle taking place within Dutch society. Another way of seeing it is as a sort of micro version of the inter-group conflict between the two parts of Dutch society. The rise of Theo van Gogh seen from a group-as-a-whole perspective is to see him as representing something for the host Dutch population. In brief, it would seem that the host community were experiencing feelings of invasion, of helplessness, of loss of identity and inability to understand and cope with the problems presented by immigrants from different cultures. At an unconscious level they sought someone to express their feelings and to challenge the Muslim approach with a view to reclaiming their identity. In other words, van Gogh was acting on the projections of the members of the host society in Holland. All in their helpless state had mobilized him to do something on their behalf and to represent their views.

In addition, by directing a film that sought to attack the Muslim part of Dutch society by concentrating on women's rights and showing a brutalized young Muslim woman while quoting from the Koran, van Gogh sought to show Muslims and their religion as uncivilized and "barbaric". Or put another way, he sought to show that Muslims were not fit to be members of a "civilized" Dutch society. We see here that van Gogh is mobilizing feelings, attitudes and stereotypes that derive from the Western constructs of Muslims and Islam. The Western construct of Muslims as mobilized by van Gogh is one which is based on centuries of viewing Muslims as untrustworthy, uncivilized, ignoring of women's rights, and followers of an autocratic and unyielding religion. As such, we can perhaps see him as a representative in a set of international relations between Western societies in their conflict with Muslim society.

To return to the analogy of seeing the tragic death of van Gogh as a sort of micro version of the inter-group conflict between the two parts of Dutch society, we also need to understand the Muslim side. The mobilization of Muslims who were prepared to kill perceived enemies of Islam when seen from a group-as-a-whole perspective is to see them also as representing something for the Muslim immigrant Dutch population. In brief, the Muslim immigrant community were experiencing feelings of helplessness, loss of identity and inability to understand and cope with the problems presented by the host community who were from different cultures. At an unconscious level they sought someone to express their feelings and to challenge the host community approach with a view to reclaiming their identity. In other words, the killers of van Gogh were acting on the projections of the members of the Muslim immigrant society in Holland. All in their helpless state had mobilized them to do something on their behalf to represent their views.

By killing this man who had directed a film that sought to attack the Muslim part of Dutch society by showing Muslims and their religion to be uncivilized and "barbaric" they sought to show that Muslims would fight to preserve their way of life. Or put another way, they sought to show that Muslims were members of Dutch society and would not be excluded as some sort of Barbarian second-class citizens. We see here that the killers are mobilizing feelings, attitudes and stereotypes that derive from the Muslim constructs of the West. The Muslim construct of the West as mobilized by the killers is one that is based on centuries of viewing Western culture as materialistic, corrupt, decadent, and immoral. They also see it as seductive, and hence stress all the more the need to resist its impact on their way of life. Increasingly Muslims attack the West for adhering to an imperfect, erroneous religion. Doubtless the Islamic world has also been influenced by many centuries of experience that affects their current thinking: from the Crusades, through the Industrial Revolution and colonization there are many factors that may affect their relatedness to the West. As such, we can perhaps see the killers as representatives in a set of international relations between Muslim societies in their conflict with Western society.

Concluding remarks

At this time, the boundary or interface between Western and Muslim cultures is of a highly dangerous and conflictual nature. It is in the nature of the "double boundary" that I described earlier in the book, where neither side is willing or perhaps able to begin to try to understand the "other". For both Western and Muslim societies the boundary is in the nature of a fixed structural conception that prevents learning. An interesting reflection on this fixed boundary is the way that Israel is building a solid wall at the boundary between Israel and Palestine; or, we might see it as at the boundary between Western and Muslim culture. Throughout history, other walls have been built that separate two polarized cultures. Usually the building is done by the members of the wealthy, "civilized" culture as a means of keeping the members of the "barbarian" culture at a distance. Walls may or may not be effective in creating a physical boundary that separates. However, walls cannot be effective in removing psychological boundaries such as that which exists between the two cultures.

The boundary is at the point that both separates and connects. Working in an uninhibited manner across the boundary can result in learning and connectedness. It can lead us as Bateson suggests to the development of binocular vision that can then enable both parties to develop a relationship whereby each does not lose their "self" concept. A relationship where each retains their own cultural beliefs but are also able to work at the process of connectedness through exploring their sameness. To get to this position requires the sort of psychological understanding that I have tried to provide throughout the book. In particular, this applies to political and other societal leaders who by their actions can either encourage members of societies to engage in ever increasing stereotyping and scapegoating of the "other", or provide the containment that enables members of societies to begin to understand the "other". This requires being the sort of understanding leader who is able to take a reflective stance and view things in a way that will not protect his or her own leadership or the unity of his or her society by demonizing others. Leadership that is based on an ability to interpret the traditional values of the society in such a way that it includes the "other", without utterly reconstructing the "other" and denying their true "otherness".

This also applies to those leaders in the military and police who have the responsibility and authority for dealing with the effects of inter-cultural conflict. Understanding beyond the actual incident in regard to any conflict that may be taking place is essential. If, for example, we take the van Gogh murder as a straightforward aggressive murderous act by some Muslim fanatic we are ignoring the true nature of the crime. Most importantly, by seeing it as a single incident we are failing to understand that such violence is never far beneath the surface and that at any given time it might break out into a conscious violent response such as happened regarding the cartoon in Denmark. Understanding at the society-as-a-whole level is also important for both police and military as a need to understand that groups and individuals may be unconsciously mobilized to take action on behalf of their society. For example, we would not be surprised if members of American and Western societies regarded the Muslim terrorists who committed the atrocities on 9/11 as inhuman. We should not be surprised therefore that members of the American military, who were almost certainly mobilized by their society, treated prisoners at Abu Graib as such. There is always the possibility that the police and military whose role is to protect society will be mobilized in similar ways. Group dynamics are extremely powerful and can lead to a collusive cruelty and violence if not understood.

Above all, at this time, is the fear of the way that youth are mobilized to do things on behalf of society, and this applies to both Muslim and Western societies. All societies are going through a period of world history that is equal to the revolutionary changes that occurred during the Industrial Revolution. Coming to terms with the death of a way of life and trying to make sense of a new way of life while fearing threats to our individual and collective identity will leave members of all societies feeling helpless and hopeless and looking for both scapegoats and saviours. As during the Industrial Revolution, violent rebellion will be ever present beneath the surface and will require little to cause it to break out into conscious reality. As was discussed in Chapter Five, for the past three years young people have been used by members of society both as scapegoats and as saviours. As we are also aware, this has resulted in rioting by young people in France and other countries. This is a highly dangerous situation that requires a deeper level of understanding by all societal leaders

This is a dangerous world where the interface or boundary between Western societal culture and Muslim societal culture is abrasive and conflictual in the extreme. As such there is a huge potential for disagreement which may continue to lead to violence. This applies to anywhere in the world where this interface exists such as: Thailand, India, Palestine & Lebanon, and Chechnia; and to any society in the world where Muslim and Western culture comes into conflict be that at a group or individual level. For the longer term, there is an urgent need for Western and Muslim leaders to actively work at the development of inter-cultural understanding. That is, a need to develop a relationship where both the West and Muslims can see each other as complete human beings who are capable of both goodness and badness. This will ensure that the boundary between the two cultures is not regarded as taboo or closed; rather, it will be an opportunity for learning where both sides can work together across the boundary to develop a new understanding that takes account of the need for a pluralistic world community. To achieve this requires that both parties develop a binocular view based on an in-depth understanding of the 'other'. In entering into a relationship it means that neither side has to lose their self concept. Indeed the nature of the relationship is a mutual recognition of sameness and difference that results in binocular vision. And this will require leadership on both sides that is based on an ability to interpret the traditional values of the society in such a way that it includes the "other", without utterly reconstructing the "other" and denying their true "otherness".

ABOUT THE AUTHOR

Lionel F. Stapley PhD, Msc is the Director of OPUS (An Organization for Promoting Understanding of Society) where he currently heads up the Listening Post Project; and an organizational consultant. Highly influential in his approach is his work as a staff member of Group Relations Conferences; and his consultancy clients include a variety of organizations in the public and private sectors, where he works with individuals, groups and sometimes with whole organizations.

He is the author of: *The Personality of the Organization: A Psychodynamic Explanation of Culture and Change* (Free Association, 1996); *"It's an Emotional Game: Learning About Leadership from the Experience of Football"* (London: Karnac, 2002); and of *"Individuals Groups and Organizations Beneath the Surface"* (London: Karnac, 2006); and co-editor with Larry Gould and Mark Stein of *The Systems Psychodynamics of Organizations* (London: Karnac, 2001), and *Applied Experiential Learning: The Group Relations Training Approach* (London: Karnac, 2004).

He is the Chair of the Editorial Management Committee of the OPUS International Journal, *Organizational & Social Dynamics*; a Fellow of the Chartered Institute of Personnel and Development

(FCIPD); a Fellow of the Chartered Institute of Management (FCIM); and a Member of the International Society for the Psychoanalytic Study of Organizations (ISPSO).

ABOUT OPUS

OPUS, an Organization for Promoting Understanding of Society, was founded in 1975 and is a registered educational charity and company limited by guarantee. Its name reflects its aim, which is to encourage the study of conscious and unconscious processes in society and institutions within it. OPUS undertakes research, organizes conferences, promotes study groups called "listening posts", and publishes bulletins and papers.

OPUS has over 200 Associates, a growing number of whom are from outside the UK. OPUS Associates are mainly professionals from a range of disciplines. OPUS also sponsors the International Journal, *Organizational & Social Dynamics*, which has a subscription base of over 500 throughout the world. In addition, OPUS organizes the Annual International Conference, "Organizational & Social Dynamics", which is a well-supported and valued event.

Further information about OPUS, can be obtained as below:

By post:	The Director, OPUS, 26 Fernhurst Road, London SW6 7JW
By phone or fax:	+44 (0)20 7736 3844
By email:	director@opus.org.uk

Or visit the OPUS website at www.opus.org.uk

For Listening Post Reports see under "Bulletins".

ABOUT AGSLO

AGSLO (A working Group for Studies of Leadership and Organization) was founded in 1974. It is organized as a foundation with the primary task to study conscious and unconscious processes in organizations and in society. Since 1975 AGSLO has yearly arranged a one-week residential group-relations conference in the Tavistock tradition and has frequently also arranged shorter conferences, seminars and listening posts. AGSLO has a Board of ten members and a Foundation Council consisting of 50 members. More information about AGSLO can be found on www.agslo.se.

Inquiries about AGSLO's activities can be made at:

The Secretary
AGSLO
c/o Gummesson
Sockenvägen 141
SE–132 46 Saltsjö-Boo
Sweden
or by telephone or fax: +46 8 18 91 19

REFERENCES

Amado, G., & Ambrose, A. (2001). *The Transitional Approach to Change*. London: Karnac.

Armstrong, D. (2005). *Organization in the Mind*. London: Karnac.

Bateson, G. (1973). *Steps to an Ecology of the Mind*. St. Albans, Herts: Paladin.

Bhaskar, R. (1975). *A Realist Theory of Science*. Brighton: Harvester.

Bion, W. R. (1961). *Experiences in Groups and Other Papers*. London: Tavistock.

Burrus, D. (1993). *Technotrends*. New York: HarperCollins.

Forester, T. (1985). *The Information Technology Revolution*. Oxford: Blackwell.

Froude, J. (1864). *Short Studies in Great Subjects*. Out of print

Hobsbawn, E. (1962). *The Age of Revolution*. London: Weidenfeld and Nicolson.

Gould, L., Stapley, L., & Stein, M. (2001). *Systems Psychodynamics of Organizations: Integrating Group Relations, Psychoanalytic and Systems Theory*. New York: Other Press.

Gould, L., Stapley, L., & Stein, M. (2004). *Applied Experiential Learning: The Group Relations Training Approach*. London: Karnac.

Kernberg, O. (1966). Structural Derivatives of Object Relationships. *International Journal of Psychoanalysis, 47*: 236–53.

Klein, M. (1955). On Identification. In *Envy and Gratitude and Other Works*. London: Virago.

Klein, M. (1959). Our Adult World and its Roots in Infancy. *Human Relations,* 12: 291–303.

Krantz, J. (2006). The Fundamentalist State of Mind in Groups and Organizations. OPUS—The Annual Eric Miller Memorial Lecture, presented on 18th March 2006 in London. Unpublished.

Kuhn, T. (1962). *The Structure of Scientific Revolutions.* Chicago, Il: University of Chicago Press.

Lewin, K. (1935). *A Dynamic Theory of Personality.* New York: McGraw-Hill.

Lewin, K. (1947). Frontiers in Group Dynamics, Parts I and II. *Human Relations, 1*: 5–1, and 2: 143–153.

Miller, E., & Khaleelee, O. (1985). Society as an Intelligible Field of Study. In M. Pines (Ed.), *Bion and Group Psychotherapy.* London: Routledge & Kegan Paul, pp. 247–254.

Miller, E. (1989). *The Leicester Model.* London: Tavistock Institute of Human Relations. Occasional Paper No.10.

Parker, G. (1988). *The Military Revolution: Military Innovation and the Rise of the West.* Cambridge: Cambridge University Press.

Pieterse, J. N. (1995). Globalization as Hybridization. In M. Featherstone, S. Lash, & R. Robertson (Eds.), *Global Modernities.* London: Sage.

Pipes, D. (2002). *Militant Islam Reaches America.* New York: Norton.

Porter, G. (1847). *Progress of the Nation.* Out of print.

Stapley, L. (1996). *The Personality of the Organization: A Psychodynamic Explanation of Culture and Change.* London: Free Association.

Stapley, L. (2005a). Report of a Birmingham Listening Post. Unpublished.

Stapley, L. (2005b). Report of a London Listening Post. Unpublished.

Stapley, L. (2006). *Individuals Groups and Organizations Beneath the Surface.* London: Karnac.

Stapley, L., & Collie, A. (2004). Global Dynamics at the Dawn of 2004. *Organizational and Social Dynamics, 4*(1).

Stapley, L., & Collie, A. (2005). Global Dynamics at the Dawn of 2005. *Organizational and Social Dynamics, 5*(1).

Stapley, L., & Cave, C. (2006). Global Dynamics at the Dawn of 2006. *Organizational and Social Dynamics, 6*(1).

Trist, E. (1990). Culture as a Psycho-Social Process. In Eric Trist & Hugh Murray (Eds.), *The Social Engagement of Social Science.* London: Free Association Books

Winnicott, D. (1971). *Playing and Reality.* Harmondsworth: Penguin.

Winnicott, D. (1988). *Human Nature.* London: Free Association.

INDEX